Reinforcement Learning for Finance

From Portfolio Allocation to Smart Execution

Victor Trex

Published by NobleTrex Press

For permissions and other inquiries, write to:
P.O. Box 3132, Framingham, MA 01701, USA

Contents

Introduction

Finance is a sequence of decisions under uncertainty. Every trade, hedge, or allocation choice balances noisy signals, evolving beliefs, and the frictions of real markets. Reinforcement learning (RL) offers a principled language for this reality: agents observe a state, act, and learn from rewards and penalties accrued over time. Yet the promise of RL in markets is not to replace financial reasoning with blind optimization; it is to formalize economic objectives, embed constraints, and harness data to improve decisions in a way that is testable, governable, and robust. This book, Reinforcement Learning for Finance: From Portfolio Allocation to Smart Execution, aims to build that bridge-uniting statistical thinking, market microstructure, and modern RL into a coherent toolkit for research and production.

The journey begins with solid footing. Quantitative and Financial Foundations gather the probability, statistics, and time-series concepts necessary to reason about noisy, autocorrelated data; the linear algebra, optimization, and stochastic processes that underpin value-function approximation and policy learning; and the securities pricing and market microstructure insights that turn abstract dynamics into executable decisions. We connect portfolio theory, risk measures, and trading frictions to the ultimate objective-realized PnL-so that what we optimize in silico aligns with what matters in production.

With the groundwork laid, Formulating Financial Decision Processes translates investment and execution problems into Markov and partially observable models appropriate for hidden liquidity and delayed information. We focus on reward engineering that encodes economic goals-risk-adjusted returns, inventory penalties, and constraint terms-so that learning signals are stable and meaningful. State representation and feature engineering draw on technical, fundamental, and cross-asset descriptors, including learned embeddings, to balance expressiveness with sample efficiency. Exploration methods are treated with particular care: in markets, data is costly and actions can move prices, so bandits and safety-aware strategies are indispensable.

Algorithms and Data Infrastructure presents the learning machinery and the plumbing that makes it credible. We progress from dynamic programming and Monte-Carlo methods to value-based deep RL, then to policy gradients and actor-critic techniques for continuous control. Model-based, offline, and safe RL methods address the realities of limited on-policy data and the imperative to respect drawdown, leverage, and turnover constraints. Throughout, market data engineering and realistic simulation environments are emphasized to avoid biases, calibrate microstructure behavior, and handle regime shifts, all while enabling reproducible experiments at scale.

Armed with these tools, Reinforcement Learning for Dynamic Portfolio Management applies them to multi-asset allocation. We design action spaces and rebalancing logic, integrate risk-aware objectives, and incorporate transaction costs, impact, and turnover control into multi-period horizons. Signal integration and feature neutralization demonstrate how to combine style premia and bespoke alpha with representation learning while mitigating unintended exposures. The theme is pragmatic alignment: agents learn policies that respect costs and risk limits, not merely maximize paper returns.

Smart Trade Execution drills down to the moment orders meet the market. We review execution benchmarks such as TWAP, VWAP, and implementation shortfall and study the schedule-risk versus market-impact trade-off. RL agents adapt order type, size, timing, and venue to limit-order-book state, queue dynamics, and latency effects. Infrastructure matters: feed handlers, clocks, and network paths influence realized slippage, and our RL environments make these influences explicit. High-fidelity, microstructure-aware simulators and sim-to-real techniques help bridge the gap between backtest and live deployment.

Finally, Evaluation, Governance, and Production Deployment formalizes how RL strategies graduate from research to reliable trading. We codify leakage-free backtesting and temporal cross-validation, then turn to online experiments-shadow trading and canary rollouts-for safe incremental exposure. Model risk, drift monitoring, and kill-switches create operational guardrails, while regulatory compliance and best-execution governance translate policies into auditable processes. We close with system architecture for training at scale and low-latency serving, and with performance and attribution reporting that communicates Sharpe, Sortino, IS/VWAP, turnover, capacity, and allocation-selection-timing effects to stakeholders.

Three principles guide the book. First, realism: objectives, costs, constraints, and latencies appear where they operate-in the reward and transition structure-rather than as afterthoughts. Second, parsimony: simple baselines remain strong competitors, so learned policies must justify their complexity against robust, transparent alternatives. Third, accountability: every result should be reproducible, stress-tested across regimes, and explainable to risk and compliance teams.

This text is written for quantitative researchers, traders, data scientists, and engineers, as well as students seeking a modern path from theory to practice. You can read linearly from foundations to deployment, or enter at the application chapters with the foundations as a reference. By the end, you will not only understand how to formulate and train RL agents for allocation and execution, but also how to validate, govern, and ship them responsibly-so that intelligent decision-making becomes a repeatable capability, not a one-off experiment.

Chapter 1

Quantitative and Financial Foundations

Before an agent can learn to trade, we must learn to describe markets precisely. This chapter turns noisy price charts into random variables and stochastic processes, abstracts portfolios into vectors and optimization problems, and reveals how microstructure and frictions distort the clean world of theory. By the end, you'll be able to translate between financial intuition and the quantitative language that modern reinforcement learning algorithms require.

1.1 Probability, Statistics, and Time-Series Analysis

In the previous chapter we described the high-level goals of reinforcement learning (RL) in finance: learn trading and allocation rules by interacting with data or realistic simulators, rather than hand-specifying strategies. To make those ideas precise, we now need a quantitative language for uncertainty and for how asset prices evolve over time.

This section develops that language. We start from probability and random variables as models of uncertain returns, move to basic statistical estimation and hypothesis testing, and then introduce time-series models that describe how returns and volatility behave across time. Throughout, we emphasize how these concepts connect directly to RL: defining the reward process, building state features, and assessing whether a learned policy truly exploits patterns or just fits noise.

Random Variables as Models of Returns

In markets, almost everything important is uncertain: tomorrow's price, next month's volatility, the future path of an index. Probability provides a way to talk about this uncertainty in a disciplined way.

Prices, Returns, and Random Variables

Consider a single asset with price P_t at time t (for example, at the close of each trading day). If we look one step ahead, P_{t+1} is unknown today. We treat P_{t+1} as a *random variable*: a numerical quantity that can take different values with certain probabilities.

For modeling trading performance and for RL, we usually work with *returns* rather than prices. A simple choice is the (discrete) simple return over one period:

$$R_{t+1} = \frac{P_{t+1} - P_t}{P_t}.$$

Here R_{t+1} is also a random variable. When we say "the expected daily return is 0.05%", or "the probability of a daily loss worse than -2% is 1%", we are making statements about the probability distribution of R_{t+1}.

Distributions, Expectation, and Risk

The *distribution* of a random return tells us how likely different outcomes are. For a continuous return, we often imagine a smooth probability density that assigns more mass to more likely values. The exact shape matters:

- The *mean* or *expected value* of R is the probability-weighted average of all possible outcomes. It summarizes the "central tendency" of returns.

- The *variance* of R, and its square root, the *standard deviation*, measure dispersion around the mean. In finance, standard deviation is a primary measure of risk (volatility).

- The *skewness* of R captures asymmetry. Positive skew means more probability of large gains than large losses; negative skew means the opposite.

- The *kurtosis* of R captures how heavy the tails are compared to a normal (Gaussian) distribution. High kurtosis means extreme events (large positive or negative returns) are more frequent than a normal model would suggest.

For an RL agent, these distributional features shape both the reward signal and the risk of policies. A policy that frequently produces small gains but occasionally incurs huge losses is very different from one with balanced tails, even if both have the same average return.

Dependence and Correlation

In multi-asset settings, we care not only about individual distributions but also about how returns move together.

- The *covariance* between two returns $R^{(1)}$ and $R^{(2)}$ measures how they co-vary around their means. Positive covariance means they tend to move in the same direction.

- The *correlation* is a scaled version of covariance that lies between -1 and 1, making it easier to interpret. A correlation near 1 implies strong co-movement; near 0 suggests weak linear dependence.

Portfolio construction and RL-based portfolio policies both rely on these dependence structures: diversification benefits, hedging, and factor exposures all hinge on correlations.

From Data to Models: Estimation and Inference

Probability gives us a theoretical language for returns. Statistics tells us how to learn about that language from finite samples of data, such as a historical price series.

Sample Moments

Suppose we observe a sequence of daily returns for an asset over T days: $r_1, r_2, \ldots, r_T$. A natural first step is to compute summaries:

- The *sample mean* return is the arithmetic average of the observed returns.
- The *sample variance* is the average squared deviation from the sample mean. Its square root is the sample standard deviation.
- Sample skewness and kurtosis describe asymmetry and tail thickness in the data, computed from powers of deviations from the mean.

These sample moments are empirical proxies for the true (unknown) mean, variance, skewness, and kurtosis. They are the simplest building blocks for both risk measures and features in RL state representations.

Parametric Models and Maximum Likelihood

Often we posit a family of distributions to model returns, and then fit their parameters. For example, we might assume that daily returns are normally distributed with unknown mean μ and variance σ^2, or that log-returns follow a Student-*t* distribution with unknown degrees of freedom.

In parametric modeling, a common estimation method is *maximum likelihood*. Conceptually, we pick the parameter values that make the observed data most probable under our model. In the normal case, maximum likelihood coincides with using the sample mean and (a slightly adjusted version of) the sample variance.

RL agents can use parametric models in several ways:

- to generate simulated returns for training in a controlled environment;
- to model the noise in rewards when designing algorithms that explicitly handle stochastic reward realizations;
- to form beliefs about the distribution of next-period returns when using model-based RL.

Confidence Intervals and Hypothesis Tests

Estimates from finite data are noisy. A sample mean of 0.05% per day is only an estimate of the true expected return. We therefore need tools to quantify uncertainty about estimates, and to test hypotheses like "does this strategy have positive alpha?"

- A *confidence interval* for a parameter (such as the mean) is a range of values that are consistent with the data at a chosen confidence level (for example, 95%). Narrow intervals mean we are more certain about the parameter; wide intervals mean the data are uninformative.
- *Hypothesis testing* compares two competing claims. For example, the null hypothesis might be that the true average return of a strategy is zero (no alpha). The alternative might be that it is nonzero. We compute a test statistic from the data and check whether it is extreme enough to reject the null at a chosen significance level.

These ideas are essential when evaluating RL strategies:

- After training a policy on historical or simulated data, we can test whether its average out-of-sample return is significantly different from that of a benchmark.
- We can assess whether apparent improvements in Sharpe ratio are larger than what could plausibly arise from random noise and multiple experimentation.

Time-Series Basics: Prices, Returns, and Stationarity

So far we have treated returns as independent draws from some distribution. Real market data, however, are observed over time, and temporal patterns matter. Time-series analysis studies sequences like $\{R_t\}_{t=1}^{T}$ with an eye toward dependence across time.

From Prices to Returns

A price series $\{P_t\}$ typically trends upward or downward over long horizons, influenced by growth, inflation, and other macro factors. This trend makes it difficult to treat prices directly as stable, stationary data. Returns, on the other hand, tend to fluctuate around a more stable central level, making them more suitable for many models.

We therefore often transform prices to returns (simple or logarithmic) as the primary time-series to model. In RL, the reward signal is typically a function of returns, not prices themselves.

Stationarity

A time series is called *stationary* if its statistical properties, like mean and variance, do not systematically change over time. More informally, a stationary series "looks the same" in distribution if we shift it a few periods forward or backward. Stationarity is a key assumption for many models and for standard inference procedures.

Returns are often *approximately* stationary over moderate periods, while prices are not. When series are not stationary, we may:

- subtract a trend or deterministic pattern,
- take differences (for example, modeling price changes rather than levels), or
- explicitly model non-stationary behavior (for example, with certain ARIMA models).

For RL, stationarity matters because typical algorithms assume that the environment's transition and reward distributions do not change over time. Strong regime shifts or structural breaks can violate this assumption and lead to degraded performance.

Autocorrelation and Partial Autocorrelation

Two simple diagnostics reveal time dependence in a series:

- The *autocorrelation function* (ACF) at lag k measures the correlation between R_t and R_{t-k}. If returns were independent over time, these autocorrelations would be close to zero for $k \geq 1$.
- The *partial autocorrelation function* (PACF) at lag k measures the correlation between R_t and R_{t-k} after removing the linear influence of intermediate lags. It helps distinguish between direct and indirect dependence.

In many liquid markets, raw daily returns show little autocorrelation, while nonlinear functions of returns, such as squared or absolute returns, exhibit strong, slowly decaying autocorrelation. This pattern is known as *volatility clustering*: periods of high volatility tend to be followed by high volatility, and quiet periods by quiet periods.

Autocorrelation structures are critical for RL because they reveal memory in the environment. If volatility clusters, then recent volatility is a useful state variable for predicting the future distribution of rewards.

Linear Time-Series Models for Returns

With these diagnostics in hand, we now consider simple models that can capture predictable components in returns. Even weak predictability can be economically important when scaled up or combined with leverage, and RL agents often rely on such structure to improve over naive baselines.

Autoregressive (AR) Models

An autoregressive model of order p, written AR(p), assumes that the current return is a linear combination of the previous p returns plus some noise. For example, in an AR(1) model, today's return depends on yesterday's return and a random shock. If the dependence is small but nonzero, there is a modest amount of linear predictability.

The ACF and PACF plots guide our choice of p: specific patterns in these functions are characteristic of AR models of certain orders. For instance, a PACF that cuts off sharply after lag 1 is consistent with an AR(1) process.

In RL, AR models can play two roles:

- as simple environment models in small-scale experiments;
- as building blocks for more complex feature engineering (for example, using lagged returns as inputs to a policy network).

Moving Average (MA) and ARIMA Models

A moving average model of order q, written MA(q), expresses the current return as a linear combination of the most recent q shocks or innovations, rather than past returns directly. Combined ARMA models allow both autoregressive and moving average components.

However, many financial series (especially in levels, like prices or log-prices) are non-stationary. To handle this, ARIMA models extend ARMA by allowing for differencing: we apply a differencing operator a certain number of times to the original series to obtain a stationary one, then fit an ARMA model to that.

For example, if log prices follow a random walk with drift, their first differences (log-returns) may be approximately stationary, and we might fit an ARMA model to those returns. In practice:

- ARIMA models are useful for one-step-ahead forecasting of returns or price changes.
- RL agents in model-based setups can use ARIMA forecasts of expected return as part of the state, or as a baseline model against

which RL improvements are measured.

Modeling Volatility and Risk Dynamics

Linear models like ARMA capture predictable patterns in the *mean* of returns. In finance, the dynamics of volatility—how risk changes over time—are just as important, particularly for risk-sensitive RL objectives.

Conditional Heteroskedasticity and Volatility Clustering

Empirically, the volatility of returns is not constant over time. Periods of calm are punctuated by periods of turmoil, during which returns are more variable. This is the phenomenon of volatility clustering mentioned earlier. In statistical terms, the variance of R_t conditional on past information changes over time in a structured way; we say the series exhibits *conditional heteroskedasticity*.

To visualize this, one often plots squared or absolute returns. Clusters of large values (in either direction) correspond to high-volatility periods. The autocorrelation of squared or absolute returns is typically strongly positive and slowly decaying, reflecting persistent volatility regimes.

ARCH and GARCH Models

Autoregressive conditional heteroskedasticity (ARCH) models, and their generalization GARCH, were developed to capture volatility clustering. In these models, today's conditional variance depends on past squared shocks and past variances. For example, in a simple GARCH(1,1) model, the conditional variance is a weighted sum of a constant, yesterday's squared shock, and yesterday's variance.

Intuitively:

- Large shocks increase tomorrow's variance, creating clusters of high volatility.

- Over time, variance tends to revert toward a long-run average level if the parameters satisfy stability conditions.

Why does this matter for RL?

- Risk-aware policies: If an agent's objective penalizes volatility or drawdowns, then state variables related to current conditional variance are crucial inputs. GARCH-type models provide a way to estimate and forecast these variances.
- Position sizing: Many trading rules adjust position sizes inversely with volatility. An RL agent might use volatility forecasts to moderate leverage in turbulent periods.
- Environment simulation: In offline or simulated RL, we can embed GARCH processes in the reward and state dynamics to create realistic training environments with clustered risk.

From Statistical Models to RL Ingredients

The tools introduced in this section feed directly into RL formulations and evaluation.

Defining the Reward Process

In RL for trading, the reward at time t is usually some function of returns, positions, and costs. For example, we might take the reward to be net portfolio return after transaction costs, or log wealth increment. The probabilistic language we have built allows us to:

- model the distribution of rewards given the state and action;
- reason about the expected cumulative reward (analogous to expected return) and its variability;
- define risk-adjusted objectives (such as penalizing high-variance or heavy-tailed reward distributions).

Constructing Informative States

Time-series models suggest which past information is useful for predicting future rewards. Typical state components include:

- recent returns and moving averages (inspired by AR/ARMA structure),
- volatility estimates or GARCH-implied conditional variances,
- indicators of current regime, built from time-series properties (for example, high vs. low volatility).

By encoding this information in the state, we give RL algorithms access to the same patterns exploited by traditional time-series models, while allowing them to learn richer, nonlinear responses.

Evaluating Policies Without Fooling Ourselves

Finally, statistical inference provides guardrails when assessing whether an RL policy truly adds value:

- We estimate the mean and variance of policy returns on out-of-sample data or in realistic simulations, and construct confidence intervals for performance metrics (such as Sharpe ratio).
- We test hypotheses comparing an RL policy to a benchmark (for example, buy-and-hold, equal-weighted allocation, or a simple ARIMA-based strategy).
- We examine residual time-series structure in the policy's returns: if strong autocorrelation or regime dependence remains, it may suggest unexploited structure or overfitting to particular episodes.

1.2 Linear Algebra, Optimization, and Stochastic Processes

In the previous section we developed a probabilistic and time-series view of returns: we treated returns as random variables evolving over time, described their distributions, and introduced basic models such as ARIMA and GARCH. We now add three more layers that are central to reinforcement learning (RL) in finance:

- a *linear-algebraic* representation of portfolios and risk,
- *optimization* as the language of rational allocation and control, and
- *stochastic processes* as models of how prices evolve dynamically.

Together, these tools let us write down the environment dynamics, the control variables (positions or orders), and the objectives that RL agents will eventually try to optimize.

Portfolios as Vectors and Markets as Matrices

Linear algebra provides a compact way to represent many financial objects you already know: portfolios, factor exposures, and covariance structures.

Portfolio Weights as Vectors

Consider n tradable assets. At a given time t, we can describe a portfolio by its *weights*:

$$w_t = (w_{1,t}, w_{2,t}, \ldots, w_{n,t})^\top,$$

where $w_{i,t}$ is the fraction of portfolio value invested in asset i (negative for short positions, positive for long positions). The weights form a vector in n-dimensional space.

Similarly, the vector of asset returns over period t is

$$r_t = (r_{1,t}, r_{2,t}, \ldots, r_{n,t})^\top.$$

The portfolio return over period t is then just the inner product:

$$R_{p,t} = w_t^\top r_t.$$

This is a simple but powerful idea: most portfolio-level quantities we care about are linear or quadratic forms in w_t. This makes them natural to express and manipulate using vectors and matrices.

Risk and Covariance as Matrices

The joint variability of asset returns is summarized by their *covariance matrix*. If Σ is the $n \times n$ covariance matrix of returns, its (i, j) element is the covariance between assets i and j. This matrix is symmetric and (under mild conditions) positive semidefinite.

Portfolio variance is then

$$\text{Var}(R_{p,t}) = w_t^\top \Sigma w_t.$$

This is a quadratic form in the weight vector. Intuitively:

- w_t tells us how much exposure we have to each asset,
- Σ tells us how much each asset varies and how they move together,
- $w_t^\top \Sigma w_t$ aggregates these into total portfolio risk.

In RL settings where the agent controls w_t (for instance, in portfolio allocation tasks), this quadratic form will appear directly in risk constraints or penalties.

Factors and Exposures

Many models treat asset returns as driven by a smaller number of underlying *factors*, such as market, value, and momentum. In a simple linear factor model, we can write

$$r_t \approx B f_t + \epsilon_t,$$

where:

- f_t is a vector of factor returns,

- B is a matrix of *factor loadings* (each row for an asset, each column for a factor),
- ϵ_t is the vector of idiosyncratic (asset-specific) returns.

Here again, linear algebra compresses information: B encodes how each asset reacts to each factor, and we can quickly compute the factor exposure of a portfolio as $B^\top w_t$.

For RL, factor representations are useful both as inputs to the state (capturing systematic risks) and as constraints or penalties (for example, limiting exposure to particular factors).

Optimization as the Language of Allocation and Control

Linear algebra gives us a way to write portfolio quantities compactly. Optimization tells us how to choose control variables—weights, positions, or actions—to achieve some objective subject to constraints.

A Basic Portfolio Optimization Problem

A classical example is mean–variance optimization. Suppose we have an estimate of the expected return vector μ and covariance matrix Σ. One basic problem is:

> Pick portfolio weights w to minimize portfolio variance $w^\top \Sigma w$ subject to reaching at least a target expected return and respecting simple constraints (such as weights summing to one).

In words, we want the *least risky* portfolio that still achieves a desired level of expected return.

This is a *quadratic optimization* problem:

- the objective $w^\top \Sigma w$ is quadratic in w,
- the constraints (sum of weights, bounds, etc.) are typically linear.

Because Σ is positive semidefinite, this problem is *convex*: any local minimum is a global minimum, and efficient algorithms exist to solve it reliably. Convexity is important because it guarantees that we can find optimal solutions without getting trapped in bad local minima.

Constraints and the Feasible Set

In practice, many constraints shape the set of admissible portfolios:

- *Budget constraint*: the sum of weights equals one for fully invested portfolios.
- *No-short constraints*: each w_i must be nonnegative.
- *Concentration limits*: individual or sector weights cannot exceed specified caps.
- *Leverage constraints*: the sum of absolute weights is bounded.

Collectively, these define the *feasible set* of portfolios. In geometric terms, the feasible set is usually a convex region in weight space (for example, a simplex or a polytope), and portfolio optimization amounts to finding the best point in this region according to our objective.

This language maps almost directly onto RL: the *action space* is the set of allowed portfolios or trades, and the *reward* is some function of expected return, risk, and costs.

Lagrangians and KKT Conditions (Conceptually)

While this book does not require you to master all the technical details of constrained optimization, it is useful to have an intuitive picture of how such problems are solved.

A common tool is the *Lagrangian*, which blends the objective and constraints into one function by introducing new variables (Lagrange multipliers) that penalize constraint violations. When the problem is convex and the constraints are well-behaved, the *Karush–Kuhn–Tucker* (KKT) conditions characterize optimality.

Conceptually:

- The Lagrangian attaches "prices" to constraints: how much does the objective worsen if we tighten a constraint?

- At the optimum, these prices balance the trade-off between improving the objective and respecting the constraints.

In RL, similar trade-offs appear when we, for example, maximize expected reward subject to a risk or leverage budget. Sometimes we embed the constraints directly in the action space; other times we add penalty terms to the reward, echoing the Lagrangian idea.

Dynamic Optimization and Control

Portfolio problems are inherently dynamic: actions today affect not only today's return but also future wealth, risk, and constraints. Dynamic optimization frameworks (like dynamic programming or stochastic control) extend static optimization across time.

RL can be viewed as a data-driven counterpart to dynamic optimization:

- *State* summarizes the relevant information (wealth, prices, volatility, positions).
- *Action* is the control (portfolio weights, orders).
- *Transition dynamics* describe how the state evolves when we take an action in a given market environment.
- *Reward* encodes immediate performance (for example, profit and loss, or risk-adjusted return).

The linear-algebraic representation of portfolios and the optimization mindset give structure to how we define state, action, and reward spaces in a principled way.

Stochastic Processes as Models of Price Evolution

Probability and time-series analysis treat returns at discrete times. Stochastic processes generalize this to entire *paths* through time, either in discrete or continuous time. They are the standard language for modeling asset prices and risk factors in modern finance.

Discrete-Time Random Walks

A simple starting point is the *random walk*. In its basic form, a random walk for prices can be written as:

$$P_{t+1} = P_t + \epsilon_{t+1},$$

where ϵ_{t+1} is a random shock (for example, independent draws from a distribution with mean zero). In terms of returns, this says that price changes are unpredictable and have no drift.

A slightly more realistic model is a random walk with drift in *log prices*. Let $X_t = \log P_t$. Then:

$$X_{t+1} = X_t + \mu + \epsilon_{t+1},$$

where μ is a constant drift term. Here, log returns are the increments of X_t and are independent and identically distributed in the simplest case.

Connecting to the previous section, such models are building blocks for ARIMA processes: a random walk in levels corresponds to stationary returns after differencing.

Markov Property and State Representation

A key concept in stochastic processes, and in RL, is the *Markov property*. A process is Markov if the future depends on the past only through the current state. That is, once we know the present, older history does not provide additional predictive power.

Many stochastic process models are Markov by construction. For example, the random walk above is Markov if the state includes the current price. More complex models, such as AR(p) processes, can be made Markov by defining the state to include the last p observations.

This is crucial for RL design:

- If we choose a state representation that makes the environment approximately Markov, standard RL algorithms are more likely to perform well.
- Time-series diagnostics (autocorrelation, volatility clustering) from the previous section help us decide which past information to include in the state so that this approximation is reasonable.

Brownian Motion and Continuous-Time Models

Moving from discrete to continuous time, the foundational process in quantitative finance is *Brownian motion*. At a high level, Brownian motion is a continuous-time process with independent, normally distributed increments. It captures the idea of continuous but highly irregular random movement.

A widely used model for equity prices is *geometric Brownian motion* (GBM). In GBM, log prices follow a random walk in continuous time: the change in log price over a small interval is the sum of a deterministic drift and a random term proportional to Brownian motion. As a result, prices themselves stay positive and have lognormal distributions over finite horizons.

GBM and its variants form the backbone of classical option pricing theory. For our purposes, they also illustrate how to connect discrete-time return models to continuous-time dynamics: daily returns can be viewed as discrete samples from an underlying continuous process.

Filtrations and Information Flow (Intuition)

Stochastic processes are always defined relative to an evolving *information set*. As time passes, we observe more of the price path, returns, and perhaps other signals. Mathematically, this evolving information is called a *filtration*.

While we will not delve into formal measure-theoretic details, it is helpful to remember:

- At each time, decisions must be based on currently available information, not on future realizations.
- Conditional expectations (such as the expected return given current information) are central objects for both pricing and control.

RL naturally fits into this picture: the agent's policy must choose actions based on the current state, which encapsulates the information available at that time.

Martingales and No-Arbitrage (Conceptually)

Another key concept is the *martingale*. A process is a martingale if its expected future value, given current information, is equal to its current value. In finance, under certain idealized conditions, discounted asset prices are modeled as martingales under a so-called risk-neutral measure. This connects to the idea of no-arbitrage: you cannot build a strategy with zero cost and strictly positive expected gain if prices follow such a martingale structure.

For RL, martingale ideas highlight an important limitation: if markets were perfectly efficient and frictionless, there would be no predictable patterns for an RL agent to exploit, except possibly by changing risk exposures. In practice, frictions, constraints, and behavioral biases create structure that RL can learn from, but martingale models provide a useful benchmark.

From Processes to RL Environments

Stochastic processes provide the backbone of RL environments for finance. Let us make the connections explicit.

Transition Dynamics

In RL, *transition dynamics* describe how the environment moves from one state to the next when the agent takes an action. In a trading context, the state might include:

- current prices or returns,
- estimated volatility or other risk indicators,
- the agent's current positions and wealth.

Given an action (for example, new target weights or specific orders), we use a stochastic process model to generate the next prices and returns. These, together with position updates and costs, determine the next state and the realized reward.

In a simulated environment, the process model is explicit: we code, for example, an AR(1) process for returns with GARCH volatility. In real markets, the process is implicit in the data-generating mechanism of the world, which we only observe via historical or streaming data.

Reward and Objective

The optimization perspective tells us to specify an objective, such as maximizing expected cumulative reward or maximizing a risk-adjusted performance measure. The stochastic process defines the distribution of future rewards under any given policy.

RL algorithms search over policies to improve this objective by learning from experience, rather than by solving the optimization problem analytically. However, the underlying mathematics is the same: linear algebra captures how positions aggregate, optimization describes what we want to achieve under constraints, and stochastic processes determine the probabilistic consequences of our decisions.

This section has introduced three pillars that will support the rest of the book:

- Portfolios and risk can be written naturally in the language of vectors and matrices. This makes portfolio return, variance, and factor exposure easy to manipulate and generalize.

- Optimization is the mathematical expression of rational allocation and control, from classical mean–variance problems to risk- and constraint-aware objectives that mirror RL rewards with penalties.

- Stochastic processes model how prices and returns unfold over time. Concepts like random walks, Markov property, Brownian motion, and martingales provide a structured way to think about market dynamics and information.

In the RL context, these tools together define the environment (through stochastic processes), the action space (through linear-algebraic portfolio representations), and the objective (through optimization criteria). The next sections will use these foundations to study pricing, market microstructure, and portfolio theory with frictions, and to show how RL agents can be embedded in those settings in a disciplined, quantitatively grounded way.

1.3 Securities Pricing and Market Microstructure

So far we have described returns statistically and modeled prices as stochastic processes. We now ask a more structural question: *why* do securities have the prices we observe, and *how* are those prices formed in actual markets?

This section proceeds in two steps:

- We start from the *pricing layer*, where the central ideas are present value, discounting, and *no-arbitrage*. Here we treat markets as if they were frictionless and perfectly competitive.
- We then zoom in to the *microstructure layer*, where prices are the result of orders interacting in an electronic limit order book. Here, frictions, queues, and execution risk matter.

For reinforcement learning (RL), the first layer clarifies how values should relate in an ideal world, giving us sanity checks and benchmarks. The second layer defines the actual environment an RL agent must interact with: the action space consists of order submissions; the state is a snapshot of the book and recent trades; and the reward depends on *execution quality*, not just mid-price changes.

Present Value, Discounting, and Cash Flows

At the most basic level, a security is a claim on a sequence of future cash flows. Pricing begins by comparing money received at different times.

Time Value of Money

A dollar today is worth more than a dollar tomorrow because money can earn interest. If the continuously compounded risk-free interest rate is r per year, then one unit of currency received at time T years in the future has a *present value*:

$$\mathrm{PV} = e^{-rT}.$$

More generally, a certain cash flow C_T at time T has present value $C_T e^{-rT}$. For multiple cash flows at times $T_1, T_2, \ldots$, we add them:

$$\text{PV} = \sum_k C_{T_k} e^{-rT_k}.$$

In simple fixed-income instruments, like zero-coupon bonds, present value and discounting alone determine price: a bond paying 1 at maturity T has price e^{-rT} under constant r. Even when r varies with maturity (a yield curve), the same principle applies: price is the discounted value of future cash flows using the relevant discount rates.

Risk and Expected Value

Most securities have *uncertain* cash flows. A stock does not promise a fixed dividend path; a corporate bond may default. To handle this, we bring in the probabilistic language from earlier chapters.

At a high level, the *economic* value of a risky cash flow is its present value under a risk-adjusted expectation. There are two main, but equivalent, perspectives:

- **Real-world (physical) measure:** We keep the actual probabilities of outcomes and adjust discount rates upward for risky cash flows.
- **Risk-neutral measure:** We adjust probabilities in such a way that, after discounting at the risk-free rate, expected prices do not offer arbitrage opportunities.

The second perspective, the *risk-neutral* one, is particularly convenient for derivatives pricing and underlies many continuous-time models.

No-Arbitrage and Pricing Relationships

The notion of *no-arbitrage* is deceptively simple:

> If a portfolio of securities produces a certain pattern of cash flows with zero cost today, then those cash flows must be worth zero in present value terms. Otherwise, there would exist a free lunch.

By comparing the cash-flow patterns of different securities and enforcing no-arbitrage, we obtain pricing relationships.

Forward and Spot Prices

A *forward contract* is an agreement entered today to buy (or sell) an underlying asset at a future date T for a predetermined price $F_{0,T}$ (the forward price). There is typically no exchange of cash today, but at time T the buyer pays $F_{0,T}$ and receives the asset.

Assume for the moment that:

- there are no transaction costs or funding frictions,
- the underlying asset pays no dividends or income before T,
- we can borrow and lend at the same risk-free rate r.

Under these assumptions, no-arbitrage implies a tight link between the current spot price S_0 and the forward price $F_{0,T}$. Consider two strategies:

- *Buy-and-hold:* Buy the asset today for S_0, finance it by borrowing S_0 at rate r, and hold until time T.
- *Forward:* Enter into a forward contract to buy the asset at time T for $F_{0,T}$, with no cost today.

Both strategies deliver the same payoff at time T: one unit of the asset, and a cash outflow equal to either the loan repayment in strategy 1 or $F_{0,T}$ in strategy 2. By no-arbitrage, these must have the same present value. This leads to the standard pricing relation

$$F_{0,T} = S_0 e^{rT}$$

in continuous compounding (or the analogous expression in simple compounding).

If this relationship did not hold, an arbitrageur could:

- lock in a riskless profit by buying the cheaper synthetic position and selling the more expensive actual one;
- or vice versa, depending on the direction of mispricing.

RL agents rarely operate directly at this level, but these relationships provide natural baselines and consistency checks for simulated environments.

Dividends, Carry Costs, and Convenience Yield

In practice, underlying assets often generate income or incur costs:

- Stocks may pay dividends.
- Commodities may incur storage costs or confer a "convenience yield" for physical holders.
- Foreign currencies involve interest rate differentials.

These features modify the no-arbitrage forward price by subtracting the present value of income and adding the present value of carrying costs. The general principle remains the same: we construct synthetic positions to replicate cash flows and enforce equality of present values.

Simple Derivatives and the Risk-Neutral View

For options and other derivatives, path-dependent and asymmetric payoffs make replication harder, but the core logic persists.

In the simplest case of a European option (exercisable only at maturity), under standard assumptions we can show:

> The current option price equals the risk-free discounted expected payoff under a risk-neutral probability measure.

Formally, let X_T be the payoff of the derivative at time T and r the risk-free rate. Then

$$\text{Price}_0 = e^{-rT}\,\mathbb{E}^{\mathbb{Q}}[X_T],$$

where $\mathbb{Q}$ is the risk-neutral measure.

You need not master the measure-theoretic details to appreciate the key point: no-arbitrage plus the ability to trade underlying assets and risk-free bonds pins down derivative prices in terms of expected discounted payoffs under a special probability measure. This is the conceptual bridge between the statistical models of returns and the prices we see in derivative markets.

From Frictionless Pricing to Real Markets

The no-arbitrage framework assumes:

- instant trading at a single market price,
- unlimited divisibility and liquidity,
- no transaction costs, bid–ask spreads, or price impact.

Real electronic markets look very different. They are *order-driven*: prices emerge from the interaction of many buy and sell *orders* in a central limit order book. For an RL agent, this microstructure is the environment it must operate in.

Order Types and the Limit Order Book

Most modern exchanges are organized as *continuous double auctions*. Buyers and sellers submit orders that are matched according to price–time priority. To navigate this environment intelligently, we must understand the basic order types and the structure of the book.

Limit Orders and Market Orders

Two foundational order types are:

- **Limit order:** an order to buy (or sell) a specified quantity at a given limit price or better. For a buy limit order, "better" means a lower price; for a sell limit order, a higher price. Limit orders can rest in the book waiting to be executed.
- **Market order:** an order to buy (or sell) a specified quantity *immediately* at the best available prices in the book. A market order prioritizes speed of execution over price certainty.

Other order types (such as stop orders or iceberg orders) are variations or combinations that control when an order becomes active or how much of it is visible.

The Limit Order Book as a Ladder of Bids and Asks

The *limit order book* is a record of all outstanding limit buy and limit sell orders not yet executed or canceled. It is typically displayed as two "ladders":

- The **bid side** shows buy orders, sorted from highest to lowest price.
- The **ask side** (or offer side) shows sell orders, sorted from lowest to highest price.

At each price level, we can see the total resting quantity. The *best bid* is the highest buy price in the book, and the *best ask* is the lowest sell price. The difference between them is the *bid–ask spread*, a key indicator of transaction cost and liquidity.

When a new limit order arrives:

- If its price is not aggressive enough to cross the spread (for example, a buy limit order priced below the best ask), it joins the book and waits.
- If its price is aggressive enough (for example, a buy limit order priced at or above the best ask), it immediately executes against the resting orders on the other side, possibly consuming multiple price levels.

When a market order arrives, it also executes immediately, walking up (for a buy) or down (for a sell) the opposite side of the book until its quantity is fully filled or the available depth is exhausted.

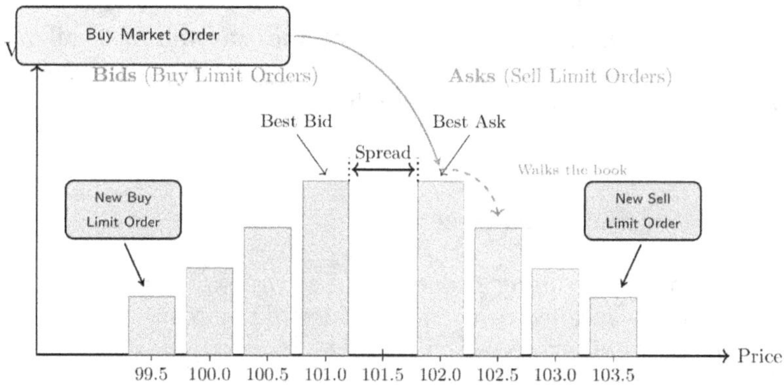

This schematic emphasizes several points:

- Volume at each price level represents queued limit orders waiting to trade.
- A market buy order consumes volume starting at the best ask and then walks up the ask ladder, potentially moving the execution price.
- New limit orders arrive and join the queue; cancellations and trades remove volume.

Microstructure Concepts: Spread, Depth, and Impact

From the limit order book, several key microstructure variables emerge. These variables form natural components of the state for an RL execution or market-making agent.

Bid–Ask Spread and Quoted Liquidity

The *bid–ask spread* is the difference between the best ask and best bid. It represents an immediate transaction cost: if you buy at the ask and immediately sell at the bid, you lose the spread.

The *quoted depth* at a given price level is the total volume available at that price. High depth at the best quotes suggests that moderate-sized market orders can be executed with little price movement, while thin depth signals fragility.

Order Flow and Imbalance

The stream of incoming orders—market orders, limit orders, and cancellations—is called *order flow*. A useful summary statistic is the *order-flow imbalance*, for example:

$$\text{Imbalance} = \frac{\text{buy volume} - \text{sell volume}}{\text{total volume}}$$

over a recent window. Strong buy imbalance may predict short-term upward pressure on prices; strong sell imbalance, the opposite.

Short-horizon RL agents, such as intraday traders or market makers, often include order-flow features as part of their state, letting them react to shifting supply and demand.

Price Impact and Slippage

A key difference between the frictionless pricing world and the microstructure world is *price impact*. Executing a large order consumes liquidity and can move prices against you.

Two related concepts are:

- **Temporary impact:** the immediate price move caused by your trade, which may partially revert as the book refills.
- **Permanent impact:** the portion of the price move that persists, perhaps because your trade conveys information about fundamental value.

In practice, traders experience *slippage*: the difference between an idealized execution price (for example, the mid-price when they decided to trade) and the actual average execution price, after walking the book and accounting for fees.

For RL, price impact and slippage must be integrated into the reward:

- A policy that naively sends large market orders might see attractive paper profits in a mid-price model, but poor realized performance once impact is accounted for.
- Conversely, a policy that places passive limit orders may earn the spread but incur execution risk (orders may not fill) and inventory risk (unwanted positions).

RL Agents in Order-Driven Markets

We now connect these microstructure ideas to the design of RL environments, states, actions, and rewards.

State Representation

A typical state for an RL trading or execution agent might include:

- a snapshot of the top levels of the order book (prices and quantities on both sides),
- recent trades (price, size, and direction),
- derived features such as spread, depth, and order-flow imbalance,
- the agent's own inventory and outstanding orders,
- volatility or risk estimates from higher-level time-series models.

The goal is to make the state *approximately Markovian*: given this information, the conditional distribution of future states and rewards does not depend heavily on longer history.

Action Space: Orders as Control Variables

In an order-driven market, the agent's control variables are *orders*. Depending on the problem, the action space may include:

- choosing between market and limit orders,
- specifying price levels for limit orders relative to the best bid or ask,
- setting order sizes,
- canceling or modifying existing orders.

In execution problems (for example, liquidating a large position over a fixed horizon), actions determine how aggressively to trade against available liquidity. In market-making problems, actions determine where to post bids and asks to earn the spread while managing inventory risk.

Reward Design: From Mid-Price to Realized P&L

Reward design must reflect the actual economic objective, not an oversimplified proxy. Common components include:

- **Realized P&L:** gains and losses from changes in position value and trade prices.
- **Transaction costs:** explicit fees and the bid–ask spread.
- **Impact costs:** modeled or measured price impact from the agent's own trades.
- **Risk penalties:** terms that discourage large inventory swings, drawdowns, or excessive variance of P&L.

For instance, an execution agent might maximize expected proceeds from selling a block of shares, minus a penalty on both execution risk (remaining inventory near the deadline) and variance of proceeds. A market-making agent might maximize a risk-adjusted spread capture, penalizing adverse selection and inventory risk.

No-Arbitrage Benchmarks and Market Frictions

Finally, the classical no-arbitrage pricing results provide useful benchmarks but must be interpreted in light of microstructure:

- In a frictionless world, any persistent deviation from no-arbitrage relationships would be instantly exploited. In real markets, frictions limit how aggressively arbitrage can be implemented.
- RL strategies that seek to exploit apparent mispricings (such as deviations between spot and forward prices) must account for transaction costs, margin requirements, and the finite speed and capacity of execution.
- Simulators that ignore these microstructure details can overstate the profitability of arbitrage-based RL policies.

Thus, when building RL environments or backtests, we should impose realistic constraints and frictions, so that the agent learns strategies that remain robust when deployed in actual order-driven markets.

This section has connected high-level pricing theory with the granular mechanics of real markets:

- At the pricing level, we saw how present value, discounting, and no-arbitrage lead to relationships among spot, forwards, and simple derivatives, and how risk-neutral valuation formalizes the link between models of returns and derivative prices.
- At the microstructure level, we described how prices are formed in an electronic limit order book, introduced key order types, and defined concepts such as spread, depth, order-flow imbalance, and price impact.
- For RL, we interpreted the limit order book as the environment, orders as actions, and realized execution quality—including slippage and costs—as the core of the reward.

These ideas set the stage for the final section of this chapter, where we integrate portfolio theory, risk measures, and trading frictions into a unified framework. There, we will see how to formulate RL objectives that are not just return-seeking, but also risk-aware and cost-conscious, bridging the gap between theoretical pricing and practical trading performance.

1.4 Portfolio Theory, Risk Measures, and Trading Frictions

The previous sections have given us the building blocks for thinking about financial decision-making:

- returns and volatility as random variables evolving over time,
- portfolios as vectors and risk as covariance matrices,
- prices as outputs of no-arbitrage relationships and order-book microstructure.

We now bring these pieces together to answer a central question for reinforcement learning (RL) in finance:

> How should we define the *objective* of an RL trading or allocation agent, taking into account both risk and trading frictions?

To do so, we proceed in three steps. First, we review classical portfolio theory in a simplified, frictionless setting. Then we introduce richer, more realistic risk measures that capture tail risk and path properties. Finally, we incorporate transaction costs and price impact, showing how they alter both optimal behavior and sensible RL reward design.

Classical Mean–Variance Portfolio Theory

Classical portfolio theory, pioneered by Markowitz, starts from a simple yet powerful observation: investors care about both expected return and risk. In a one-period setting, with n assets, we denote:

- μ as the vector of expected asset returns,
- Σ as the covariance matrix of asset returns,
- w as the vector of portfolio weights.

The expected portfolio return and variance are then:

$$\mathbb{E}[R_p] = w^\top \mu, \qquad \text{Var}(R_p) = w^\top \Sigma w.$$

The Efficient Frontier

Suppose investors dislike risk but like return. In this stylized setting, an investor faces a trade-off: higher expected return generally comes with higher variance. A portfolio is *efficient* if there is no other portfolio with:

- higher expected return for the same variance, or
- lower variance for the same expected return.

The set of all such efficient portfolios forms the *efficient frontier*. Geometrically, when we plot portfolio variance on the horizontal axis and expected return on the vertical axis, the efficient frontier is the upper-left boundary of all achievable portfolios. Every point on the frontier corresponds to a different set of weights w, and investors with different risk tolerance will choose different points along this frontier.

In an RL context, the efficient frontier provides:

- a benchmark for what is achievable in a static, one-period world without trading frictions;
- a target region: an RL portfolio policy should strive to produce average return–risk combinations that are competitive with efficient frontier portfolios.

Risk-Return Preferences and Utility

Mean–variance analysis implicitly assumes investors have quadratic utility or returns are normally distributed. In both cases, expected return and variance fully summarize preferences. While real investors often care about more than variance (for example, skewness and drawdowns), mean–variance theory remains a useful first-order approximation and a natural starting point for RL reward shaping.

Even in more general settings, we can think of the investor as maximizing some *utility* of final wealth or of the stream of returns. In practice, we often approximate such utilities with risk-adjusted performance metrics, like the *Sharpe ratio*:

$$\text{Sharpe ratio} = \frac{\mathbb{E}[R_p - R_f]}{\sqrt{\text{Var}(R_p - R_f)}},$$

where R_f is the risk-free rate. RL objectives frequently resemble Sharpe-like ratios, combining mean and variance of returns.

Beyond Variance: Modern Risk Measures

Variance penalizes both upside and downside deviations from the mean equally. However, investors typically care more about large losses than large gains. This motivates richer risk measures tailored to the shape and path of returns.

Value at Risk (VaR)

Value at Risk at level α over a given horizon is a quantile-based measure. Informally:

> VaR_α is a number such that, with probability α, losses will not exceed that amount over the specified horizon.

For example, a one-day 99% VaR of 2% means that on 99% of days, the portfolio is not expected to lose more than 2% of its value. VaR is widely used for regulatory and internal risk reporting, but has well-known limitations:

- It says nothing about the size of losses beyond the VaR threshold (how bad the 1% worst days are).
- In some settings, it can be non-convex, making it awkward for optimization.

For RL, VaR can appear as a constraint or penalty, but its quantile nature makes differentiability and learning more subtle.

Expected Shortfall (ES) and Tail Risk

Expected Shortfall (also called Conditional VaR) addresses some of VaR's issues. At level α, ES is the *expected loss given that the loss exceeds the* VaR_α. In words, ES summarizes the severity of tail events, not just their frequency threshold.

ES is more sensitive to rare but catastrophic events, and it has desirable mathematical properties (in particular, it is a coherent risk measure). This makes it a better candidate for optimization and for risk-aware RL:

- We can penalize policies that occasionally generate very large losses, even if their average performance is strong.
- ES-based objectives encourage strategies that are robust in the tails, which is particularly important when training RL agents on limited historical data.

Drawdowns and Path-Dependent Risk

Investors also care about *paths* of returns, not just their distribution at a single horizon. A key path-dependent metric is *maximum drawdown*: the largest peak-to-trough decline in the portfolio value over a given window.

For example, a strategy that compounds at a high average return but occasionally suffers 50% drawdowns may be unacceptable for many investors. Maximum drawdown captures this concern directly.

In RL, drawdowns can be integrated into the reward in several ways:

- adding explicit penalties when current drawdown exceeds a threshold;
- constraining policies to keep drawdown below a maximum level;
- modifying the utility to be more loss-averse after large declines (state-dependent risk aversion).

These design choices directly influence how aggressively the agent trades and scales capital, particularly in volatile environments.

Factor Risk and Exposures

Beyond scalar risk measures, we also care about *which* risks a portfolio is taking. Factor models decompose returns into exposures to underlying risk drivers (such as market, size, value, and sector factors). Factor exposures can be seen as additional state variables and constraints:

- A portfolio may be required to stay market-neutral (zero exposure to the broad market factor).
- Sector or style score exposures may be capped.

For RL, factor exposures are natural components of both state (what risk is the policy currently taking?) and constraint sets (what risk should it avoid?).

Trading Frictions: Costs and Price Impact

Classical portfolio theory assumes that we can costlessly rebalance portfolios. Real trading is different. Every trade incurs *frictions* that erode performance and reshape optimal behavior.

Types of Transaction Costs

We distinguish several common types of costs:

- **Proportional costs:** Costs that scale with traded volume or notional. These include the bid–ask spread and broker commissions. If we buy at the ask and later sell at the bid, we effectively pay the spread twice.
- **Fixed costs:** Costs incurred per trade regardless of size (for example, ticket fees). These discourage frequent small trades.
- **Market impact costs:** Implicit costs from moving the price against oneself when trading larger sizes, as introduced in the microstructure section.

These costs make rapid rebalancing and aggressive trading less attractive. In fact, they can entirely wipe out the gains of a high-turnover strategy that looks profitable in a cost-free backtest.

Simple Impact Models

To build intuition, consider a simple parametric model of temporary price impact. Suppose the mid-price before we trade is p. If we buy quantity q, the average execution price might be:

$$p + \gamma q,$$

where γ is an impact coefficient capturing how sensitive prices are to our trade size. Larger trades incur a higher average purchase price. Symmetrically, large sells push the price down and reduce average sale price.

This simple linear impact model is not perfect, but it captures key intuition:

- Impact increases with trade size.
- Impact turns the act of trading itself into a source of risk and cost.

For RL, such models are often embedded in simulated environments, allowing agents to learn that aggressive trading is costly and that splitting orders over time may reduce impact.

From Frictionless Rebalancing to Optimal Trading

Under no transaction costs, the mean–variance optimal portfolio is static: if estimates of μ and Σ do not change, the investor can hold the same $w^\star$ indefinitely.

With frictions, optimal strategies become *dynamic and state-dependent*:

- There is a *no-trade region* around the target weights. Small deviations from the ideal portfolio are not worth correcting because the cost of trading outweighs the benefit of precise rebalancing.
- When holdings drift too far from target, it becomes optimal to trade back toward the center of the no-trade region.
- The size of the no-trade region depends on transaction cost parameters, volatility, and investment horizon.

This picture aligns closely with RL: the optimal policy in a frictional world is inherently dynamic and must weigh future benefits of changing the portfolio against immediate costs and risks.

Embedding Risk and Frictions into RL Rewards

We now connect these ideas explicitly to RL problem formulation. In RL, we choose:

- *state space:* what the agent observes,
- *action space:* what decisions the agent can take,
- *reward function:* what we ask the agent to maximize.

Risk measures and trading frictions influence all three, but they enter most directly through the reward.

Net P&L as the Base Reward

The natural starting point is *net profit and loss (P&L)* over a time step. If w_t is the portfolio before trades, w_t' after trades, r_{t+1} the vector of returns, and C_t total trading cost incurred at t, then a simple one-step reward could be:

$$R_{t+1} = (w_t')^\top r_{t+1} - C_t.$$

Here:

- $(w_t')^\top r_{t+1}$ is the gross portfolio return,
- C_t captures proportional costs, fixed costs, and impact.

By subtracting costs explicitly, we ensure the agent cannot ignore trading frictions. Over many steps, the agent maximizes expected cumulative net P&L.

Risk-Adjusted Rewards

Maximizing raw P&L tends to produce high-risk strategies, especially when training environments are limited and overfitting is a concern. To align with portfolio theory, we can adjust rewards for risk:

- **Variance penalty:** Subtract a term proportional to instantaneous or recent variance of returns. This is the RL analogue of trading off mean and variance.
- **ES or tail penalty:** Penalize large negative returns more heavily, for example by applying a nonlinear loss function that grows faster for large drawdowns.
- **Drawdown penalty:** Subtract a penalty when cumulative drawdown exceeds a threshold, encouraging the agent to avoid deep and prolonged losses.

Mathematically, these adjustments modify the effective utility the agent is maximizing. Practically, they can greatly improve stability and investor acceptability of learned policies.

Penalizing Turnover and Overtrading

High turnover amplifies transaction costs and impact. To discourage unnecessary trading, we can explicitly penalize changes in positions. For instance, define the trade vector $\Delta w_t = w'_t - w_t$. A turnover penalty can be built from:

- the sum of absolute changes in weights, or
- the notional traded volume.

Including such penalties in the reward serves two purposes:

- It approximates real trading costs when a full microstructure model is unavailable or too expensive to simulate in detail.
- It encourages parsimonious, more interpretable strategies that rely on robust signals rather than constant churning.

Constraints as Hard Limits vs. Soft Penalties

Risk measures can be incorporated either as *hard constraints* or as *soft penalties*:

- Hard constraints restrict the action space or state space. For example, limiting leverage, capping position sizes, or forbidding trades that would push ES beyond a limit.
- Soft penalties, akin to Lagrangian multipliers, keep the action space large but make riskier actions less rewarding. For example, adding a term $-\lambda \cdot \text{ES}$ or $-\lambda \cdot \text{Drawdown}$ to the reward.

In RL, hard constraints must often be enforced by the environment (for example, rejecting invalid actions), while soft penalties are easier to encode directly in the reward. A practical design balances both: use hard constraints to ensure safety and regulatory compliance, and soft penalties to guide the policy toward desirable trade-offs within the safe region.

Putting It Together: A Quantitative Template

Let us summarize how the elements of this section yield a concrete template for RL in portfolio and trading problems:

- **From portfolio theory:** use mean–variance ideas to define target risk–return trade-offs. The efficient frontier and Sharpe ratio serve as benchmarks and inspirations for reward design.
- **From modern risk measures:** include tail risk (VaR/ES), drawdowns, and factor exposures as additional dimensions of performance. These become constraints, state variables, or components of the reward.
- **From trading frictions:** model transaction costs and price impact explicitly. Reward is based on *realized* net P&L, not just changes in mid prices or theoretical values.
- **From RL:** treat portfolio weights or trade sizes as actions; include risk states (volatility, ES, drawdown, factor exposures) and cost states (recent turnover, liquidity conditions) in the observation; and optimize a risk-aware, cost-adjusted cumulative reward.

With this template, we move from an abstract "maximize expected return" view to a grounded, implementable RL formulation that respects the realities of financial markets and the preferences of real investors. Subsequent chapters will build on this foundation, illustrating how specific RL algorithms can be tailored to portfolio allocation, market making, and smart execution under these risk and friction-aware objectives.

Chapter 2

Formulating Financial Decision Processes

Before any learning algorithm can make money-or lose it-you must decide what the "game" actually is. In finance, that means turning vague goals like "beat the benchmark with limited drawdowns" into precise, sequential decision problems: what information the agent sees, which levers it can pull, how the market responds, and what exactly counts as success. This chapter shows how to cast portfolio allocation, market making, and execution as Markov or partially observable decision processes, design economically meaningful rewards, and build state and feature representations that let RL agents learn efficiently from scarce, noisy market data-all while exploring the market without burning PnL.

2.1 Markov and Partially Observable Decision Models for Finance

In reinforcement learning, everything starts from how we describe a sequential decision problem. Before we worry about algorithms, neural networks, or training tricks, we must answer a simpler question:

What exactly is the decision-maker seeing, deciding, and affecting over time?

In finance, that decision-maker might be:

- a portfolio allocator rebalancing among many assets,
- a trader slicing a large order across venues and time,
- a market maker continuously posting quotes while managing inventory risk.

All of these can be framed as *sequential decision processes*. In this section, we formalize this using Markov Decision Processes (MDPs) and Partially Observable MDPs (POMDPs), and we show how these abstractions fit naturally with market uncertainty and limited information.

From financial problems to decision processes

Any sequential decision problem has a few core ingredients:

- a description of the situation the agent is in (the *state*),
- a set of choices (the *actions*),
- rules describing how situations evolve when actions are taken (the *dynamics or transitions*),
- and a notion of performance (rewards and, later, objectives).

In finance, the raw world is messy: prices stream in from many venues, liquidity appears and disappears, and information arrives with delays. The role of problem formulation is to compress all this into a structured model that is rich enough to capture key economic trade-offs but simple enough to be tractable.

The MDP and POMDP formalisms are the standard tools for this. They do not assume a particular algorithm; instead, they give us a clean language for expressing:

- what the agent knows at each time,
- what it can do,
- and how its actions influence future opportunities and risks.

Markov decision processes in a trading context

An MDP models a fully observable environment: at each decision time, the agent sees the current *state* of the world. Intuitively, the state should summarize all relevant information from the past so that, given the state, we do not need to know the entire history.

The Markov property

The *Markov property* is the key simplifying assumption:

> Given the current state and action, the probability distribution of the next state does not depend on earlier states or actions.

In words: if the state has been chosen cleverly enough, the past matters only through its effect on the current state. For a trading agent, that might mean that future price moves, order fills, and inventory changes depend on:

- the current prices and order book,
- current inventory, cash, and open orders,
- and perhaps a few recent returns or volatility estimates,

but not on *exactly* what happened two hours ago beyond what these variables already encode.

An MDP is then built from:

- a state space (all possible states),
- an action space (all possible actions),

- transition dynamics (how states evolve given actions and randomness),
- and a reward rule (how we measure short-term performance).

We will momentarily focus on structure rather than equations, to keep the intuition clear.

States, actions, and transitions for portfolio allocation

Consider a daily portfolio allocation problem across N assets plus a cash position. Each trading day t, the allocator chooses portfolio weights for the next day. A simple MDP formulation might be:

State. At the close of day t, the state may include:

- current portfolio weights across assets and cash,
- latest prices or log-prices for each asset,
- recent returns or technical indicators (e.g., 5- and 20-day moving averages),
- factor-based signals (value, momentum, carry, quality, ...),
- risk model outputs (estimated volatilities and correlations).

This state vector should capture what is necessary to forecast the distribution of next-day returns and portfolio risk.

Action. The action could be:

- a new target weight vector (subject to long-only or leverage constraints), or
- the trade list: how many shares to buy or sell of each asset and how much to move into or out of cash.

Transition. Between day t and $t + 1$:

- asset prices move according to the underlying stochastic process of returns,

- trades are assumed to execute at or near observable prices (for this simple example),
- new portfolio weights are determined mechanically from executed trades and price moves,
- signals and indicators are updated based on new prices.

Together, these rules determine how the environment moves from one state to the next. In practice, we estimate or simulate these transitions using historical data or a market simulator.

States, actions, and transitions for optimal execution

Now consider intraday execution of a large sell order in a single stock, over a fixed horizon (say one hour, discretized into 5-minute intervals). Here, the agent's role is not to take market risk for profit, but to trade at good prices while controlling footprint and execution risk.

State. At each decision time, the state could include:

- remaining inventory to sell,
- current mid-price and bid-ask spread,
- depth at best bid and ask, and perhaps a few levels of the limit order book,
- recent trade sizes and directions (buy vs. sell pressure),
- time remaining in the execution horizon.

Action. The agent chooses an execution action, such as:

- a market order size,
- a limit order size and price offset from the mid,
- a decision to wait and not trade this interval.

Transition. Over the next 5 minutes:

- limit orders may be (partially) filled depending on market order flow,

- the mid-price and spread evolve according to supply and demand, including the agent's own impact,
- remaining inventory decreases with executed volume,
- time-to-go decreases by one step.

Here, the episode ends when either the entire parent order is executed or the time horizon ends. This boundary condition is part of the MDP specification.

Market making as an MDP

For market making, the agent posts bid and ask quotes and manages its inventory risk.

State. A typical state vector might contain:

- current inventory and cash,
- current bid and ask prices and the mid-price,
- a summary of recent order flow (buy vs. sell imbalance, arrival rates),
- volatility and spread estimates over the last few minutes.

Action. The agent chooses:

- the distance of bid and ask quotes from the mid-price,
- and possibly skew (tightening one side, widening the other) based on inventory.

Transition. Between decisions:

- counterparties hit or lift the agent's quotes, changing inventory and cash,
- the mid-price and spread fluctuate due to broader market activity,
- order flow statistics and volatility estimates update.

With these ingredients, we obtain a clean MDP description: at each time step, the market maker observes a state, chooses quote parameters, and then experiences random fills and price moves that produce a new state and a trading profit or loss.

Partial observability and why MDPs are not always enough

Real markets are rarely fully observable. Behind visible prices and top-of-book quotes lie many hidden factors:

- latent liquidity in dark pools or hidden orders,
- unobserved trading intentions of large players,
- regime shifts in volatility or correlation that are not directly seen,
- delays and noise in data feeds or internal systems.

An MDP assumes that the agent sees the full state. In many financial settings, this is unrealistic. Instead, the agent only sees an *observation*, which is a noisy or incomplete view of an underlying *true state*. This motivates the Partially Observable MDP (POMDP).

From MDP to POMDP: adding hidden variables

A POMDP extends an MDP by distinguishing between:

- the *true state* of the world (including hidden variables),
- what the agent can actually see (the *observation*).

The true state might include:

- all observed variables (prices, inventory, etc.),
- plus latent quantities such as:
  - a hidden volatility regime (calm vs. turbulent),
  - hidden order book depth beyond the visible levels,

– latent order flow imbalance that will influence future trades.

The agent does *not* observe these latent variables directly, but it can infer them imperfectly from past observations and actions. This introduces an information-processing layer on top of the MDP dynamics.

Belief states: summarizing uncertainty about hidden variables

In theory, optimal decisions in a POMDP can be made by keeping track of a *belief state*: the agent's probability distribution over the true state, given all past actions and observations. Intuitively, the belief state is:

> "What the agent currently thinks might be true about the market, and how confident it is."

The belief state is updated recursively:

- observe new market data (prices, trades, quotes),
- combine this with prior belief and knowledge of the transition dynamics,
- produce a new belief about hidden variables (for example, that volatility has likely jumped).

In practice, explicitly maintaining a full probability distribution is often impossible in rich financial environments. Instead, we rely on approximations.

Illustrative MDP vs POMDP schematic for trading

To make the distinction concrete, Figure shows side-by-side diagrams of an MDP and a POMDP formulation for a trading task. On the MDP side, the agent directly observes the full state, including inventory and all relevant market variables. On the POMDP side, some components of the state are hidden (for example, true liquidity or latent volatility). The agent only receives partial observations and maintains an internal belief or filter to approximate the hidden information.

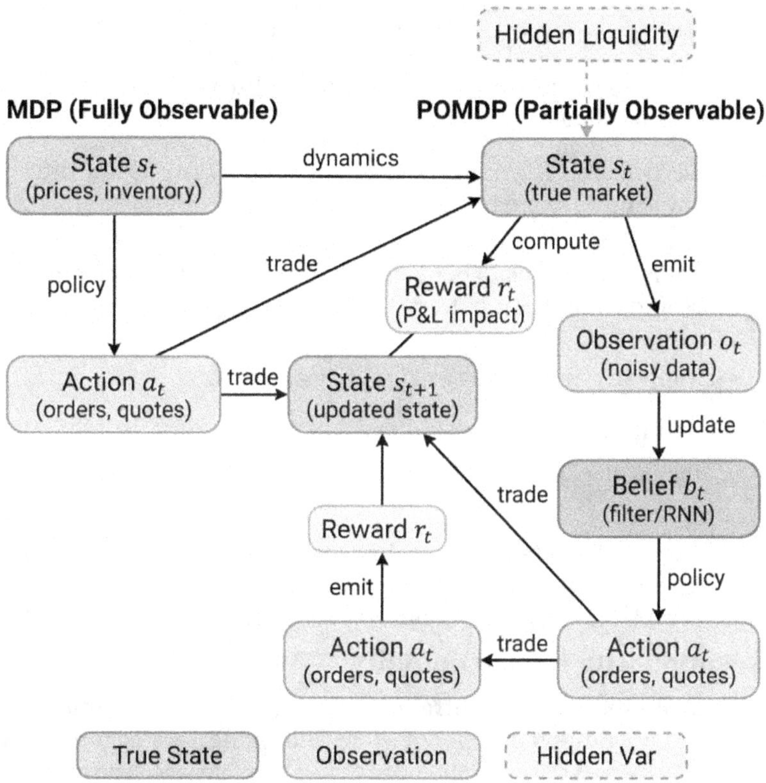

Examples of partial observability in finance

Let us revisit our three canonical tasks and see where POMDP structure naturally appears.

Portfolio allocation under hidden regimes

A daily allocator may suspect that markets move through regimes: low-volatility bull markets, high-volatility crises, sideways ranges, and so on. Returns and correlations behave differently in each regime, but the regime itself is not directly observable.

One POMDP view is:

- The true state includes both observable variables (prices, factors, current portfolio) and a hidden regime label.
- The observation includes only the observable variables; the regime is latent.
- The transition dynamics govern both how regimes switch and how returns behave within each regime.

The agent may construct a belief about the current regime from recent volatility and correlation patterns, using for example:

- simple moving-average volatility estimates,
- a hidden Markov model filter,
- or a recurrent neural network that ingests recent returns.

The belief (or the filter's internal state) can be fed as part of the RL state representation, providing an approximate sufficient statistic for decision making in a partially observable world.

Execution with hidden liquidity

In optimal execution, a central challenge is *hidden liquidity*. Public quotes show a limited number of levels; additional resting interest may exist in dark pools or in hidden portions of book orders. The agent does not know exactly how much will execute at a given price until it actually trades.

A POMDP perspective is:

- The true state includes visible book levels, plus true depth at each price (visible + hidden), including dark pool availability.
- The observation includes only the visible portion and possibly the agent's recent fill outcomes.
- The agent uses these observations to infer how much liquidity is likely to be available at different price levels and venues.

Here, a belief about hidden liquidity might be approximated using:

- exponential smoothing of observed fill ratios,
- Bayesian models of depth conditional on book snapshots,
- or neural networks trained to predict expected fill size based on recent order flow.

These belief summaries then become part of the RL state, allowing the agent to adapt its execution style (more aggressive vs. more patient) to inferred liquidity conditions.

Market making with unobserved order flow imbalance

A market maker cares deeply about incoming order flow: if buy orders dominate, the maker risks accumulating a short inventory as it sells into demand, and vice versa. While recent trades are observed, the underlying pressure from large institutional programs or hidden orders is not.

In a POMDP formulation:

- The true state includes an unobserved order flow imbalance variable that influences the likelihood of future buys vs. sells.
- The observation includes actual executed trades and quote changes.
- The agent maintains a belief about this latent imbalance, which influences how it skews its quotes to manage inventory risk.

In practice, the belief might be represented by a few carefully chosen features (such as cumulative net buy volume over a short window) or by the hidden state of a recurrent network. Again, the RL state then consists of observable data plus these belief features.

Practical approximations to POMDPs in RL for markets

While POMDPs are conceptually appealing, exact belief-state planning is often infeasible in high-dimensional, continuous financial environments with complex dynamics. Fortunately, RL practice in finance has developed a set of pragmatic approximations that capture the spirit of POMDPs without the full mathematical burden.

Augmenting the state with short histories

The simplest approach is to relax strict Markovianity and include a short history of past observations and actions directly in the state. For example, instead of feeding only the latest price and volume, we might include:

- the last k mid-prices or returns,
- the last k spreads and depths,
- recent trade signs and sizes.

This allows the agent to infer patterns such as trends or mean reversion, and to estimate hidden variables (like volatility) implicitly.

Though this technically violates the minimal-state ideal, it often restores an approximate Markov property in a higher-dimensional space that is still manageable for modern RL algorithms.

Filtering with simple statistical models

Another approach is to run a separate filter that maps past observations to a low-dimensional set of inferred variables. For example:

- Use an exponentially weighted moving average (EWMA) of squared returns as a proxy for latent volatility.
- Use a Kalman filter to track a latent factor that drives returns.
- Use an online estimator of fill probability per venue as a proxy for hidden liquidity.

The RL agent then treats these filtered variables as part of the observable state. In effect, we are hand-crafting a belief state using classical time series tools.

Learned belief states with recurrent networks

When the environment is complex and we have sufficient data and compute, we can let the function approximator learn its own internal representation of beliefs. Recurrent architectures (such as LSTMs or gated recurrent units) or transformers are natural candidates.

In this setup:

- At each decision time, the agent receives the current observation vector and its previous hidden state.
- The recurrent network updates the hidden state, which implicitly summarizes past information.
- The policy and value functions condition on this hidden state, effectively treating it as a belief.

From the point of view of the RL algorithm, the problem becomes an MDP on an extended state space that includes both the raw observation and the learned hidden state. From the point of view of the underlying market, we are approximately solving a POMDP.

When is an MDP formulation adequate? When is a POMDP necessary?

Not every financial problem needs a full POMDP treatment. As a rule of thumb:

MDP formulations are often adequate when:

- The agent operates at high frequency and sees rich microstructure data (deep book, trades, quotes) with low latency.
- The main sources of uncertainty can be captured well by observable variables and simple summary statistics (e.g., short-horizon volatility and order flow).
- The goal is to react quickly to current conditions, with relatively short planning horizons.

In such cases, adding more hidden-structure modeling can add complexity without much benefit. A carefully engineered state vector may be enough to satisfy the Markov property for practical purposes.

POMDP formulations become important when:

- Key drivers of risk and return are inherently hidden or slow-moving (e.g., regimes, macroeconomic states, large hidden liquidity).
- Observations are sparse or delayed (e.g., trading on end-of-day prices, or in opaque over-the-counter markets).
- The agent must reason about uncertainty in a structured way (e.g., weighing exploration vs. exploitation when true payoffs are ambiguous).

In these cases, explicitly modeling beliefs, whether by filters or recurrent nets, can significantly improve performance and robustness.

Defining episode boundaries and horizons

A final practical element of MDP/POMDP formulation is deciding where episodes begin and end. This choice encodes important economic and operational assumptions.

Portfolio allocation. Episodes might:

- correspond to fixed horizons (for example, a rolling 1-year investment horizon),
- or be continuous, with a discount factor used to weight distant outcomes less.

Execution. Episodes commonly:

- start when a parent order is received,
- and end when the order is fully executed or a time limit is reached.

Market making. Episodes might:

- be defined over a trading day, resetting overnight,
- or use a long horizon with periodic inventory or risk-limit resets.

The horizon interacts with the state and reward design: if inventory must be flat at the end of an episode, then the state should include time-to-go so that the agent can plan to wind down positions.

In this section, we reframed financial problems as Markov and partially observable decision processes. For each of portfolio allocation, optimal execution, and market making, we identified:

- **State:** what the agent needs to know to forecast future outcomes and risks,
- **Action:** what the agent can control (allocations, orders, quotes),
- **Transitions:** how markets and inventories evolve given actions and randomness,
- **Observations vs. true state:** where information is incomplete or noisy.

We saw that an MDP description is often sufficient when observable data are rich and the main uncertainties are well captured by engineered features. When hidden variables like liquidity, regimes, or order flow imbalance matter, a POMDP view is more appropriate, and beliefs must be approximated via filters, histories, or learned representations.

This decision-process foundation underpins everything that follows: in the next sections, we will turn to the question of what objectives these agents should optimize (reward engineering), and what information should be included in the state to make learning feasible and economically meaningful (state representation and feature engineering).

2.2 Reward Engineering for Economic Objectives

In the previous section we focused on *formulation*: how to cast portfolio allocation, trading, and execution problems as Markov or partially observable decision processes, specifying states, actions, and transitions. Once that scaffolding is in place, a natural question arises:

> Given this decision process, *what exactly do we want the agent to maximize?*

In reinforcement learning, the answer is encoded in the *reward function*. The reward is not just a bookkeeping device; it is the economic contract between you and the agent. If you get the contract wrong, the agent will dutifully optimize the wrong thing: it may overtrade, take hidden tail risks, or exploit loopholes in your environment model.

This section develops a systematic approach to turning economic objectives—return, risk, cost, and constraints—into reward functions that are numerically stable and behaviorally realistic.

From economic objectives to RL rewards

Classical finance typically phrases objectives at a relatively high level:

- maximize expected terminal wealth or cumulative profit and loss (PnL),
- maximize risk-adjusted return (for example, Sharpe ratio),
- minimize execution cost relative to a benchmark (such as VWAP or arrival price),
- respect position limits, leverage bounds, or regulatory constraints.

Reinforcement learning, by contrast, works with *per-step rewards*. At each time t the environment emits a scalar signal r_t, and the agent maximizes some discounted or undiscounted sum of these rewards. Our task is therefore to bridge the gap:

- take the high-level economic goal,
- decompose it into quantities that can be computed at each decision step,
- combine these quantities into a scalar reward that faithfully reflects the goal, while remaining numerically well-behaved.

To keep the exposition accessible, we will emphasize verbal definitions and simple algebra rather than heavy notation.

PnL-based rewards: the starting point

The most direct starting point is *incremental PnL*. At time t, we can compute how the agent's wealth changed since the previous decision:

- mark the portfolio to market at $t-1$ and at t,
- subtract direct transaction costs (commissions, fees, spread losses),
- the difference is the increment in portfolio value.

A natural per-step reward is then

$$\text{reward}_t = \text{PnL}_t,$$

the raw change in wealth. This aligns directly with the goal of maximizing expected cumulative PnL.

Advantages. This definition is:

- conceptually simple and closely tied to economic outcomes,
- additive over time, which matches the additive nature of many RL returns,
- compatible with both portfolio and execution settings.

Limitations. However, pure PnL rewards can be problematic:

- **High variance.** Financial returns are noisy, especially at high frequency. The reward sequence can be extremely volatile, making learning slow or unstable.
- **No explicit risk control.** Maximizing expected PnL does not penalize strategies that take large, unstable bets with severe drawdowns or crash risk.
- **No cost or impact awareness.** If the simulator does not faithfully account for transaction costs and impact, the agent may learn to churn the portfolio to harvest noise.

To address these issues, we enrich the reward with additional terms that capture risk, cost, and constraints.

Benchmark-relative rewards

Economic objectives are often relative, not absolute. A portfolio manager may be evaluated versus:

- a benchmark index (for example, S&P 500),
- a risk-free asset,
- or a custom reference portfolio.

In such cases, a more appropriate reward is *excess return* or *relative PnL*. For a portfolio allocator with benchmark wealth V_t^{bmk} and agent wealth V_t, a per-step reward can be defined as:

$$\text{reward}_t = (V_t - V_{t-1}) - (V_t^{bmk} - V_{t-1}^{bmk}).$$

This is the incremental outperformance versus the benchmark. Over an episode, the sum of these rewards equals the total value added relative to the benchmark.

For execution tasks, similar ideas appear in:

- **Implementation shortfall:** difference between the realized execution price and the decision (arrival) price.

- **VWAP slippage:** difference between the agent's average price and a volume-weighted average price benchmark during the execution window.

The reward might be defined as the negative of slippage or shortfall, so that *higher reward equals better execution.*

Why benchmark-relative rewards help. They:

- focus the agent on adding value beyond what could be achieved by passive exposure or naive execution,
- reduce the influence of broad market moves that are outside the agent's control,
- can improve stationarity: the reward distribution may be more stable across regimes when common components are subtracted.

Incorporating risk: variance and drawdown penalties

Economic objectives almost always involve trade-offs between return and risk. RL, however, traditionally cares only about expected return unless we modify the reward.

Two intuitive ways to introduce risk into the reward function are:

Variance or volatility penalties

We can discourage highly volatile PnL by subtracting a term related to squared returns or squared PnL increments. For example, a per-step reward might be:

$$\text{reward}_t = \text{PnL}_t - \lambda_{risk} \cdot \widehat{\sigma}_t^2,$$

where $\widehat{\sigma}_t^2$ is a rolling estimate of variance (or squared return) and λ_{risk} is a tunable penalty weight.

Conceptually, this is a per-step proxy for maximizing a risk-adjusted quantity, similar in spirit to the Sharpe ratio. The agent is rewarded for PnL, but penalized for strategies that produce unstable returns.

Drawdown-related penalties

Human investors care strongly about *drawdowns*: drops from a peak in wealth. We can include this concern by tracking:

- the running maximum of wealth over the episode,
- the current drawdown (peak minus current wealth, possibly scaled).

Then the reward can include a term such as $-\lambda_{dd} \cdot \text{drawdown}_t$. This encourages policies that avoid or quickly recover from large drawdowns.

Practical tips. When adding risk penalties:

- start with small penalty weights and gradually increase,
- monitor whether the agent learns to "freeze" and avoid trading altogether (overly conservative),
- check sensitivity: if slight changes in λ_{risk} or λ_{dd} radically change behavior, your environment or reward scaling may need adjustment.

Encoding costs and market impact

Trading costs and market impact are central in execution and high-frequency trading. If your reward ignores them, the agent will often learn pathological behaviors:

- excessive turnover,
- rapid "ping-pong" trading in and out of positions,
- quote placement that maximizes fills but also maximizes adverse selection.

To prevent this, the reward must explicitly subtract:

- **Direct costs:** commissions, fees, and fixed per-trade costs.

- **Spread costs:** half-spread losses when crossing the book with market orders.
- **Market impact:** price moves caused by the agent's own trades, often modeled as a function of trade size relative to local liquidity.

A generic per-step reward for an execution agent might look like:

$$\text{reward}_t = -\text{slippage}_t - \lambda_{risk} \cdot \text{inventory\_risk}_t.$$

Execution example. Suppose an agent is executing a sell order. At time t it sells q_t shares at an average price p_t^{exec}, while the benchmark price is p_t^{bmk} (e.g., arrival price). The cost incurred relative to the benchmark is $(p_t^{bmk} - p_t^{exec})q_t$ (positive if the agent sells below benchmark). The reward could be:

$$\text{reward}_t = -(p_t^{bmk} - p_t^{exec})q_t - \lambda_{inv} \cdot \text{remaining\_inventory}_t.$$

The first term encourages trading at or above the benchmark; the second discourages leaving too much inventory until late in the horizon.

Market making example. For a market maker, costs arise from adverse selection and inventory risk. A reward might be:

$$\text{reward}_t = \text{spread\_capture}_t - \lambda_{inv} \cdot \text{inventory}_t^2 - \lambda_{trade} \cdot \text{trading\_volume}_t.$$

Here:

- *spread_capture* is the revenue from buying at bid and selling at ask,
- the inventory-squared term penalizes large directional exposure,
- the volume term discourages excessive quote aggressiveness that leads to too many trades.

Soft constraints via penalties

Real trading systems operate under constraints:

- maximum leverage or gross exposure,
- position limits per asset,
- capital or margin requirements,
- regulatory constraints such as short-selling limits.

In classical optimization, constraints can be treated with Lagrange multipliers or by projecting back into the feasible set. In RL, we have similar options:

- **Hard constraints:** disallow invalid actions entirely. For example, truncate an action that would exceed a position limit.
- **Soft constraints:** allow violations but penalize them in the reward.

Soft constraints are often more convenient when building simulators and when you want the agent to learn to *avoid* the edges of the feasible region rather than frequently hitting them.

A typical design is to subtract a penalty proportional to the degree of violation. For example, if $L_{\max}$ is a leverage limit and L_t is current leverage, a penalty term might be:

$$\text{penalty}_t^{lev} = \lambda_{lev} \cdot \max\{0, L_t - L_{\max}\}^2.$$

The squared term grows quickly for large violations, strongly discouraging behavior that would be operationally unacceptable.

Reward shaping: making sparse objectives learnable

Some economic objectives are naturally *sparse* or *delayed*. For example:

- A long-horizon allocator might care only about terminal wealth at the end of a year.
- An execution algorithm might be judged solely on the final average execution price.

If we give a non-zero reward only at the end of the episode, learning becomes difficult: many long sequences of actions produce the same delayed reward, and it is hard for the agent to assign credit or blame to specific decisions.

Reward shaping refers to modifying the reward signal to provide denser feedback, while ideally preserving the same optimal policy.

Incrementalizing terminal objectives

For a terminal wealth objective, instead of:

- $r_t = 0$ for $t < T$, and $r_T = V_T$,

we can use per-step wealth changes:

- $r_t = V_t - V_{t-1}$ for each t.

The sum of stepwise rewards equals $V_T - V_0$, so optimizing cumulative reward is equivalent to optimizing terminal wealth. But now the agent receives feedback every period.

Shaping with potential functions

In some cases, we can add terms to the reward that depend on a potential function of the state, such that the optimal policy remains unchanged. Intuitively, we are free to add "hints" that depend on where the agent is, as long as they telescope over time and do not bias the long-run objective.

In practice, designing exact potential-based shaping functions in finance can be tricky. Nonetheless, the guiding principle is: when you introduce shaping terms, verify that you are not inadvertently incentivizing behaviors you do not want, such as frequent oscillation between states that yields shaping rewards without true economic benefit.

Scaling and numerical stability

Even a well-conceived reward can fail in practice if its *scale* is inappropriate. RL algorithms are sensitive to the magnitude and distribution of rewards.

Common issues.

- **Very large or very small rewards.** If rewards are in the hundreds of thousands, neural network gradients may explode or require very small learning rates. If they are tiny, gradients may vanish.
- **Extremely heavy tails.** Rare but huge PnL shocks can dominate learning and destabilize policies.
- **Heterogeneous scales.** Combining PnL terms (in dollars), risk penalties (dimensionless), and cost penalties (basis points) without normalization can make it hard to tune penalty weights.

Practical remedies.

- Normalize PnL by an appropriate scale, such as initial capital, average daily volume, or volatility.
- Consider clipping extreme rewards during training (while monitoring that this does not distort behavior unacceptably).
- Standardize components before combining them, for example by dividing each term by a rolling standard deviation.
- Use separate logging of raw economic quantities (unscaled PnL, drawdowns, etc.) alongside the scaled reward to ensure the agent's apparent improvement corresponds to real economic improvement.

Case-study sketches: rewards by problem type

To make the design process concrete, we now sketch typical reward formulations for three canonical tasks. These are not the only valid designs, but they illustrate how the same principles combine differently by context.

Long-only portfolio allocation

Economic goal: maximize excess return over a benchmark with controlled risk and turnover.

A plausible per-step reward (for daily decisions) is:

$$\text{reward}_t = \underbrace{\text{excess\_PnL}_t}_{\text{return}} - \underbrace{\lambda_{risk} \cdot \widehat{\sigma}_t^2}_{\text{risk penalty}} - \underbrace{\lambda_{tc} \cdot \text{transaction\_cost}_t}_{\text{cost penalty}}.$$

Here:

- *excess_PnL* is the portfolio's PnL minus benchmark PnL,
- $\widehat{\sigma}_t^2$ is a short-horizon variance estimate, capturing risk,
- *transaction_cost* includes explicit fees and estimated impact costs.

Over short horizons, the agent learns that taking some active risk can pay off, but extreme risk and unnecessary trading are discouraged.

Execution of a single large order

Economic goal: minimize implementation shortfall and inventory risk within a fixed horizon.

At each decision step:

$$\text{reward}_t = -\text{shortfall\_increment}_t - \lambda_{inv} \cdot \text{remaining\_inventory}_t - \lambda_{temp} \cdot \text{temporary\_impact}_t.$$

- *shortfall_increment* measures degradation of execution price relative to arrival price.
- *remaining_inventory* penalty pushes the agent to finish on time.
- *temporary_impact* term discourages overly aggressive participation that moves the price too much.

The trade-off between finishing early (reducing timing risk) and trading gently (reducing impact) is encoded directly in the relative sizes of λ_{inv} and λ_{temp}.

Market making

Economic goal: earn spread revenue while keeping inventory and tail risk under control.

A generic reward might be:

$$\text{reward}_t = \text{realized\_spread\_PnL}_t - \lambda_{inv} \cdot \text{inventory}_t^2 - \lambda_{gamma} \cdot \text{price\_risk}_t.$$

- *realized_spread_PnL* captures the difference between execution prices and mid-prices.
- *inventory-squared* penalizes directional imbalances.
- *price_risk* may approximate exposure to volatility (for example, inventory times volatility estimate).

By observing how the learned policy behaves under different penalty weights, we can align the agent's aggressiveness and skew with desk-level risk preferences.

Testing and iterating on reward functions

Reward engineering is rarely perfect on the first attempt. Before committing to large-scale RL training, it is good practice to *unit-test* your reward function:

- **Analytic sanity checks.** Given a few simple hypothetical scenarios (for example, "no trades," "always long the market," "immediate execution of full order"), compute the cumulative reward and verify that scenarios you prefer economically indeed yield higher reward.
- **Simulated baseline policies.** Run basic heuristic policies (buy-and-hold, TWAP execution, symmetric quotes for a market maker) in your environment and compare their average reward and economic metrics.

- **Sensitivity analysis.** Vary penalty weights and observe whether behavior changes smoothly or chaotically. Large discontinuities often signal design or scaling issues.

Importantly, treat the reward as part of the *modeling process*, not as a fixed given. As you gain experience with the environment and policy behaviors, you may refine the reward to better capture your true economic objectives.

In this section, we translated high-level financial goals—return, risk, cost, and constraints—into concrete reward functions suitable for reinforcement learning:

- Starting from incremental PnL and benchmark-relative performance,
- we incorporated risk through variance and drawdown penalties,
- added explicit terms for costs and impact to discourage overtrading,
- encoded constraints via soft penalties,
- and used reward shaping to make delayed objectives learnable.

We also emphasized practical considerations: scaling, numerical stability, and sanity-checking reward functions with simple policies before training sophisticated agents.

With a clear reward definition in place, we can now return to the question of *information*: in the next section we will discuss state representation and feature engineering, examining what signals and summaries of the market should be provided to the agent so that it can effectively optimize the carefully designed rewards described here.

2.3 State Representation and Feature Engineering

In the first section of this chapter we described how to cast financial problems as MDPs or POMDPs by specifying states, actions, and transitions. In the second section we turned economic goals into reward functions. We now address the third pillar of problem formulation:

> *What information should the agent see at each decision time, and how should that information be encoded?*

This is the question of *state representation*. In practice, it is one of the most important determinants of whether an RL approach in markets will succeed. A well-designed state:

- contains the information needed to predict rewards and state transitions,
- is compact enough to learn from the available data,
- and is constructed in a way that avoids subtle biases and data leaks.

We will build up the topic gradually: from raw market data, to engineered features and factor signals, and then to learned representations that can replace or augment hand-designed features.

From raw data to state: observables, features, and factors

It is useful to distinguish three layers of information:

- **Raw observables:** what the trading system directly receives from the world.
- **Engineered features:** transformations of raw data that highlight patterns, such as technical indicators or volatility estimates.
- **Factors and higher-level signals:** more abstract variables that capture persistent drivers of return, risk, or liquidity.

Raw observables

Depending on the time scale and the problem, raw observables may include:

- *Prices and returns:* last traded price, bid and ask quotes, mid-price, and their recent history.
- *Volumes:* traded volume over recent intervals, order sizes, and cancellations.
- *Order book snapshots:* prices and quantities at multiple bid and ask levels.
- *News or macro data:* sentiment scores, economic releases, or corporate events.
- *Internal variables:* portfolio holdings, cash, margin utilization, risk limits.

These observables are the raw material from which we construct the state. Feeding them directly to a learning algorithm is sometimes possible (especially with modern deep networks), but often inefficient. Many raw variables are redundant and highly correlated; others are on very different scales.

Engineered features

Engineered features apply relatively simple transformations to raw data to capture economically meaningful patterns. Common examples include:

- **Technical indicators:** moving averages, momentum over fixed windows, relative strength indices, Bollinger bands.
- **Volatility and correlation estimates:** rolling standard deviations, realized volatility, pairwise correlations.
- **Microstructure features:** order book imbalance, bid-ask spread, queue position, trade sign imbalance.

- **Calendar features:** time-of-day, day-of-week, month-of-year, distance to market open or close.

These features provide the agent with compact summaries of recent dynamics: trend vs. mean-reversion, high vs. low volatility, tight vs. wide spreads, and so on.

Factors and higher-level signals

In portfolio management, factor models describe asset returns as driven by a smaller set of systematic components, such as:

- value (cheap vs. expensive),
- momentum (winners vs. losers),
- quality and profitability,
- carry or term structure in fixed income and FX,
- size, industry, and style factors.

For RL, these factors are not actions themselves; they are part of the state. They encapsulate information about expected returns and risks that is often more stable over time than raw price changes.

In an execution or intraday trading context, higher-level signals might be:

- a latent measure of order flow toxicity,
- a regime label (calm, trending, stressed),
- or an internal signal indicating whether a particular alpha strategy is currently "on" or "off."

A layered view of state construction

Figure shows a conceptual pipeline from raw data to the final state vector that is passed to the RL agent. Each layer compresses and restructures information, with the aim of delivering an informative yet tractable representation.

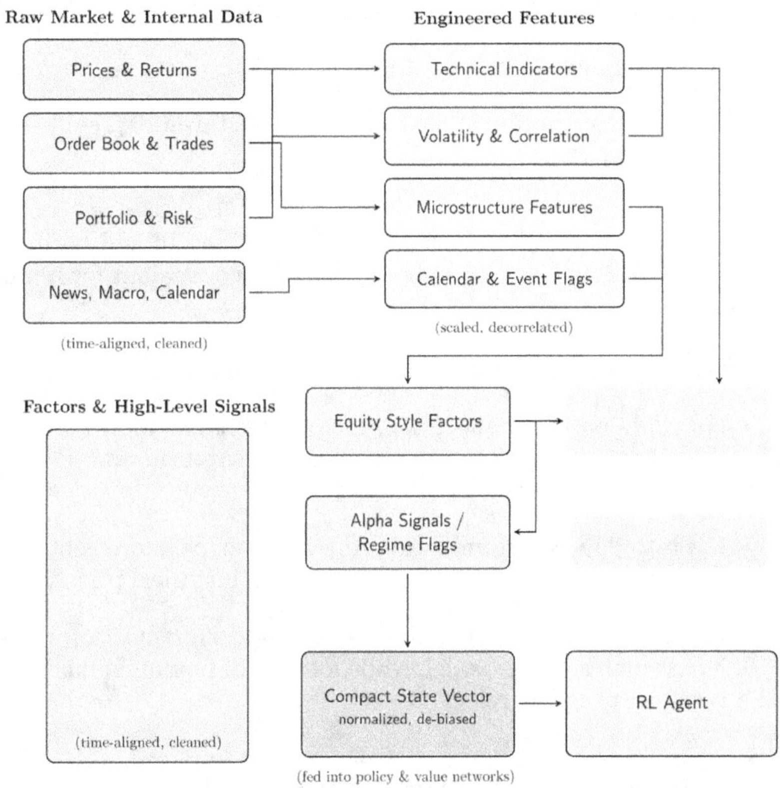

This layered view mirrors common practice in quantitative finance: data engineering and factor modeling sit between the raw market feed and any downstream optimization or learning algorithm.

Design principles for good state representations

The art of state design is to choose variables that are *informative* but not *overly complex*. Several principles help guide this process.

Focus on predictive sufficiency

For a given problem, ask:

> What do I need to know at time t to predict:
>
> - the distribution of next states (prices, inventory, etc.),
> - and the distribution of next rewards?

Variables that materially affect these distributions should be in the state. Variables that are redundant, or merely convenient for human interpretation, can often be omitted.

Examples:

- For daily portfolio allocation, factor exposures and risk model outputs are often more predictive of future returns and risk than raw closing prices.
- For intraday execution, local order book shape and recent trade imbalance are more relevant than distant historical prices.
- For market making, inventory, spread, and short-horizon volatility estimates are essential, while long-term fundamentals of the asset are usually irrelevant.

Avoid look-ahead and survivorship bias

A subtle but critical requirement is that the state must be *causally valid*: it may use only information that would have been available at decision time in real trading.

Two common pitfalls are:

- **Look-ahead bias:** using future information when constructing current features. For example, computing volatility using returns from $t+1$ to $t+20$ and then feeding that to the agent at time t.
- **Survivorship bias:** using only assets that survive to the end of the sample when building features or factor exposures. This can give a falsely optimistic picture of strategies that hold "survivors."

To avoid these issues:

- Build features using only past and present data relative to each decision time.
- Incorporate delistings and corporate events realistically in the data pipeline.
- Where necessary, shift labels and features to match the information that would have been known at each time.

Normalize and decorrelate features

Raw financial variables can vary hugely in scale: prices may be in hundreds of dollars, volumes in millions of shares, probabilities between zero and one. Neural networks and many RL algorithms perform better when inputs are roughly centered and have similar scales.

Practical steps include:

- Standardizing features (subtract mean, divide by standard deviation) over a rolling window or training set.
- Scaling volumes and trade sizes by average daily volume or by a per-asset liquidity metric.
- Converting prices to returns or log-returns, which are more stationary.
- Applying simple decorrelation techniques (such as principal component analysis) if features are extremely redundant.

Normalization must be done without leaking future information: statistics used for scaling should be estimated using only past data or a training subset.

Control dimensionality

A naive approach of including every conceivable feature yields a huge state vector. High-dimensional states have two main drawbacks:

- They demand more training data to estimate policies and value functions reliably.
- They increase computational cost and complicate debugging.

Dimension reduction can be achieved through:

- feature selection based on domain insight,
- aggregating related variables (for example, summarizing the order book by a few imbalances and depth measures rather than dozens of levels),
- projecting large factor sets onto a smaller number of principal components or cluster representatives,
- or using learned embeddings, which we discuss later.

The goal is not to minimize dimension at all costs, but to carry only as much information as is justified by the data and the problem.

Example state designs by problem type

To ground these ideas, we outline typical state designs for three representative tasks.

Daily portfolio allocation

For a multi-asset portfolio rebalanced daily, a common state design might include:

- **Asset-level features:**
  - recent returns over multiple horizons (1, 5, 20 days),
  - moving-average indicators (short- vs. long-window),
  - realized volatility estimates,
  - factor exposures (value, momentum, size, sector).
- **Portfolio-level variables:**
  - current portfolio weights,
  - current and forecast risk metrics (volatility, tracking error),
  - leverage or gross/net exposure.
- **Context variables:**
  - macro indicators or regime flags,
  - calendar features (month-end, pre-holiday).

These are typically arranged as a large vector, possibly with a structured organization (for example, grouping features by asset and type) that neural networks can exploit.

Intraday trading

For an intraday trading agent taking speculative positions, the state tends to focus on short-horizon dynamics:

- short-window returns or price changes (for example, over the last few seconds or minutes),
- order book imbalance (total bid minus total ask volume at top levels),
- spread and depth at best quotes,

- recent trade counts and volume split between buys and sells,
- local volatility estimates,
- current position and unrealized PnL,
- time-of-day and distance to session close.

Here, the state may also include a short history of observations to help approximate partially observed variables like latent order flow.

Execution and smart order routing

For an execution agent slicing a large order across time and venues, the state would typically comprise:

- remaining inventory and original order size,
- time remaining to the execution deadline,
- per-venue liquidity metrics (top-of-book depth, estimated fill probabilities),
- recent execution outcomes (fills vs. cancellations),
- current market price and spread,
- internal risk or participation-rate limits.

In multi-venue settings, per-venue features may be arranged in a consistent order across the state vector to allow the agent to learn cross-venue patterns.

Learned representations and embeddings

Hand-crafted features can be powerful, especially when combined with domain expertise. However, they have limitations:

- They may miss subtle patterns in joint dynamics across many variables.

- They require substantial manual design and maintenance as markets evolve.

Learned representations use machine learning models to compress complex observations into lower-dimensional vectors, which then serve as components of the RL state.

Autoencoders for cross-sectional embeddings

In a cross-sectional setting (many assets at a given time), an autoencoder can be trained to:

- take in a vector of asset features (for example, fundamentals, technical indicators),
- compress it through a bottleneck layer,
- and reconstruct the original features at the output.

The bottleneck layer acts as a learned factor representation, capturing major sources of variation in the data. The RL state for portfolio allocation might then include:

- the compressed representation for each asset,
- plus a few hand-crafted risk and constraint variables.

These learned "factors" can adapt as the structure of the universe changes, potentially offering more flexibility than static factor models.

Recurrent networks for temporal embeddings

In time series settings, recurrent neural networks (RNNs), gated recurrent units (GRUs), and LSTMs can learn to summarize recent history into a hidden state that functions as a compact belief about the current market condition.

A typical pattern is:

- feed sequences of past raw observations (prices, order book snapshots) into a recurrent encoder,
- at each decision time, extract the current hidden state,
- treat that hidden state as part (or the entirety) of the RL state vector.

This approach is especially helpful in partially observable environments. The recurrent hidden state serves as an approximate belief over latent variables (such as volatility regimes or hidden liquidity), much like the belief state in a POMDP.

Transformers and path embeddings

For richer path-dependent structures, transformers can be applied to windows of historical observations. Self-attention mechanisms learn which parts of the past are most relevant for predicting future dynamics. The transformer outputs a fixed-size embedding summarizing the recent path, which can then be provided to the RL agent as a state component.

Contextual variables and regime information

Finally, state representations can include contextual variables that change more slowly than intraday prices but still influence optimal behavior:

- **Regime indicators:** labels from clustering or hidden Markov models that classify periods into "normal," "volatile," or "crisis" regimes.
- **Macro environment:** interest rates, credit spreads, economic surprise indices.
- **Business context:** fund-level risk appetite, temporary restrictions, capital inflows or outflows.

Including such variables helps the agent learn how its policy should adapt across different environments. For example, a market-making strategy might choose tighter spreads in calm regimes and wider spreads in stressed regimes, even if local microstructure features look similar.

Putting it all together

Designing state representations for RL in finance is a multi-step modeling exercise:

- Start from the problem definition and reward: what does the agent need to know to make good decisions with respect to this objective?
- Identify relevant raw data sources and ensure they are cleaned, synchronized, and free from forward-looking information.
- Construct engineered features and factors that reflect known economic patterns: technical indicators, risk model outputs, microstructure measures.
- Normalize, rescale, and, when appropriate, reduce the dimensionality of these variables.
- Where beneficial, augment hand-crafted features with learned embeddings that capture complex cross-sectional or temporal structure.
- Test the resulting state design with simple baseline policies and sanity checks before deploying expensive RL training runs.

The goal is not to discover a single "best" state representation, but to find a design that is rich enough to support good performance, simple enough to train reliably on available data, and grounded in sound financial reasoning. In the final section of this chapter, we will see how these state representations interact with exploration and data-efficient learning strategies, completing the bridge from problem formulation to practical RL deployment in financial markets.

2.4 Exploration, Bandits, and Data-Efficient Learning

Up to this point in the chapter, we have treated the environment and the agent's objective as if they were already known. We defined decision processes (states, actions, transitions), engineered reward functions aligned with economic goals, and designed state representations that capture relevant information about markets.

In practice, however, the agent must *learn* how rewards depend on its actions and on the state. This requires *exploration*: trying actions whose consequences are not yet well understood. In finance, exploration is costly and risky. Every trade used to "learn" is a real trade, with real slippage, fees, and potential losses.

This section focuses on how to collect *informative* experience in markets while controlling these costs. We will:

- contrast classical exploration strategies with the realities of trading,
- introduce bandit and contextual bandit formulations as data-efficient approximations,
- discuss safety-aware exploration in live markets,
- and explain how off-policy learning and historical data help reduce the need for expensive online experimentation.

Exploration vs. exploitation in financial decision processes

Reinforcement learning agents face a fundamental tension:

- **Exploitation:** choose the action that seems best based on current knowledge.
- **Exploration:** choose actions that may appear worse now but could lead to better information and higher long-run performance.

In a typical RL benchmark (such as a video game), exploration is "free": the agent can try wildly different actions without real-world consequences. In contrast, in finance:

- exploration incurs *transaction costs* and *market impact*,
- poor exploratory trades can cause *drawdowns* and reputational risk,
- and the environment is *non-stationary*: what you learn today may not hold tomorrow.

Exploration policies must therefore be more disciplined than in synthetic benchmarks. The goal is not only to learn quickly, but to learn *safely*.

Classical exploration strategies and their limitations

Standard RL texts introduce simple exploration rules such as:

- **ε-greedy:** with probability $1 - \varepsilon$, choose the best-known action; with probability ε, choose an action at random.
- **Softmax/Boltzmann exploration:** choose actions stochastically with probabilities increasing in their estimated value, but not deterministically.

While these strategies are useful as conceptual starting points, applying them naively in trading is problematic:

- Randomly choosing between "long," "short," or "flat" positions in significant size can create uncontrolled risk.
- In highly liquid markets, random large orders induce unnecessary costs and impact.
- In illiquid markets, they can produce extreme price moves and regulatory issues.

We rarely want exploration that simply "shakes up" the policy everywhere. Instead, we prefer exploration that is:

- **Targeted:** focused on states or actions where the agent is uncertain.
- **Context-aware:** informed by features and market conditions.
- **Risk-aware:** respecting position, leverage, and loss limits at all times.

These desiderata naturally lead us to *bandit* and *contextual bandit* formulations as building blocks.

Bandits as simplified financial decision problems

A multi-armed bandit is a simple sequential decision problem where:

- at each round, the agent chooses one of several "arms" (actions),
- receives a stochastic reward depending only on that arm,
- and the environment has no explicit state dynamics (no notion of tomorrow's state being influenced by today's action).

In trading terms, bandit formulations are appropriate when:

- temporal dependence is weak or can be ignored at the decision horizon,
- or we wish to focus on learning a mapping from current context to immediate reward, without modeling long-run inventory and state evolution.

Examples of bandit-like problems in finance include:

- **Strategy selection:** at the start of each day, allocate capital among a small set of pre-defined alpha strategies, each treated as an "arm."

- **Venue selection:** for each child order, choose one of several execution venues or dark pools.
- **Quote placement variants:** select among a few discrete quoting configurations (tight, medium, wide spread) for a market-making system.

The key advantage of bandit models is that they offer well-studied, *data-efficient* exploration rules such as upper confidence bounds and Thompson sampling.

Upper Confidence Bound (UCB) and Thompson sampling

Two widely used bandit exploration strategies are:

Upper Confidence Bound (UCB)

UCB-style methods maintain estimates of the mean reward of each arm and an uncertainty measure (for example, based on how many times the arm has been tried). At each round, the agent selects the arm with the highest *upper* confidence bound:

estimated mean reward + exploration bonus

Arms with little data have larger uncertainty and therefore higher exploration bonuses, encouraging the agent to try them. Arms that consistently underperform, even after exploration, are eventually discarded.

In trading, UCB can be used for:

- adaptively allocating flow across venues, favoring those with historically better price and fill quality but still occasionally testing others,
- choosing execution aggressiveness levels (e.g., aggressive, neutral, passive) based on observed slippage results.

Thompson sampling

Thompson sampling treats the unknown reward of each arm as a random variable with a prior distribution. At each round:

- sample a plausible reward value for each arm from its posterior distribution,
- pick the arm with the highest sampled reward.

This naturally balances exploration and exploitation: arms with more uncertainty are more likely to look good in some samples, and thus be chosen, while arms with strong evidence of being inferior are rarely sampled as the best.

In finance, Thompson sampling fits neatly with Bayesian views of uncertainty about strategy performance or venue quality. It can be particularly appealing when we want an interpretable notion of "confidence" or when we wish to incorporate prior beliefs (for example, about new venues being initially less trusted).

Contextual bandits: using features without full RL complexity

Plain bandits ignore context: they assume that the reward of each arm is fixed (or changes in a way independent of the current state). This is too restrictive for most financial applications, where market conditions at decision time strongly influence returns, costs, and fill probabilities.

Contextual bandits extend bandits by introducing features observed at each decision (the context). At time t:

- the agent observes a feature vector x_t capturing current conditions (for example, volatility, spread, liquidity),
- chooses an action a_t (e.g., select a venue, a strategy, or an aggressiveness level),
- and receives a reward r_t that depends on both x_t and a_t.

The agent's goal is to learn a function mapping (x_t, a_t) to expected reward. This is mathematically simpler than full RL because we do not model how (x_t) evolves as a function of actions; we just treat each round as an independent contextual prediction problem.

Contextual bandits are especially useful when:

- we can summarize the relevant market information in a feature vector,
- the action we choose has only modest long-term impact on future states (or we are willing to ignore that dependence),
- and we want a principled way to explore across actions *conditioned on context*.

Examples of contextual bandit formulations

Adaptive allocation across alpha strategies. Suppose a fund has several alpha models, each suggesting trade signals. At the start of each day, the context includes:

- recent performance of each alpha,
- current volatility regime,
- macro indicators.

The action is a choice of capital allocation across these alphas, subject to risk limits. The reward is the next-day PnL or risk-adjusted PnL. A contextual bandit can learn how to weight each alpha as a function of the context, exploring more when uncertain and settling on effective combinations in familiar regimes.

Execution venue and order type selection. For each child order, the context includes:

- current spread and depth at each venue,
- historical fill probability and slippage by venue,
- order size relative to typical trade size.

The action is to choose a venue and order type (for example, market order vs. limit order). The reward reflects realized execution quality. A contextual bandit can then learn which venue and order type work best under different liquidity and volatility conditions.

Safety-aware exploration in live trading

Even with bandit and contextual bandit frameworks, we must enforce risk and cost controls during exploration. Several design patterns help:

Constrained action spaces

We can limit exploration to a *safe envelope* around a known baseline policy. For instance:

- allow exploratory shifts in allocation weights only within a small deviation from a benchmark portfolio,
- permit execution agents to vary participation rates within a bounded range,
- restrict market makers to quote within certain distance bands from the mid-price.

These constraints can be encoded directly in the action space, ensuring that exploratory actions cannot violate hard risk or regulatory limits.

Gradual policy updates

Instead of deploying a radically new RL policy at once, use:

- **Policy mixing:** trade a convex combination of the baseline policy and the learned exploratory policy, initially heavily weighted toward the baseline.
- **Ramp-up schedules:** gradually increase the fraction of flow governed by the learned policy as confidence in its performance grows.

These techniques reduce the impact of any single erroneous exploratory decision.

Uncertainty-aware action selection

If the learning algorithm provides uncertainty estimates (for example, via Bayesian models, ensembles, or bootstrap methods), the agent can:

- avoid large position changes in regions of the state-action space where uncertainty is high,

- treat high-uncertainty actions as candidates for small-scale experiments rather than full-scale deployment.

In contextual bandits, this appears naturally in UCB or Thompson sampling. In full RL, similar ideas can be implemented with ensemble Q-networks or Bayesian policy approximations.

Off-policy learning and “cheap” exploration from historical data

Live exploration is costly. Fortunately, financial markets generate vast amounts of historical data: order books, trades, quotes, and the actions of past strategies. We can treat this data as a source of *off-policy* experience: observations of what happened under some other policy (for example, a previous algorithm or a human trader), rather than our current one.

Off-policy RL and related techniques allow us to:

- estimate the value of new policies using data collected under old policies,
- improve policies without interacting with the live environment,
- pre-train policies and value functions before deployment, reducing the need for risky online exploration.

However, using historical data effectively requires care:

- **Coverage:** historical actions must sufficiently cover the state-action space we care about. If the old policy never tried certain regions, off-policy estimates there will be unreliable.
- **Non-stationarity:** markets evolve. Policies trained purely on old regimes may underperform when conditions change.
- **Confounding:** historical actions reflect specific human or algorithmic decision rules, which may be correlated with unobserved variables. This complicates causal interpretation.

Despite these challenges, off-policy methods (such as fitted Q-iteration, off-policy actor-critic, and importance-weighted policy evaluation) are key tools for making RL in finance more data-efficient and safer.

When to use bandits vs. full RL

It is helpful to think of bandits and RL as points on a spectrum of temporal complexity:

- **Bandits and contextual bandits** are appropriate when each decision is effectively myopic: the main question is "what is the best choice *right now* given context?" and the effect of current actions on future states is either negligible or can be safely ignored.
- **Full RL (MDPs/POMDPs)** is needed when actions have significant, state-dependent long-term effects, such as building up inventory, influencing price paths via impact, or interacting with slow-moving risk constraints.

A pragmatic workflow is:

1. Start with a contextual bandit approach whenever possible, especially for problems like strategy weighting and venue selection. This gives you a data-efficient way to learn context-dependent decisions with relatively simple models and exploration rules.
2. As evidence accumulates that temporal dependencies matter (for example, that today's execution choice materially affects tomorrow's price or inventory), gradually enrich the model into a full RL treatment, using the learned bandit policy as a strong baseline or initialization.

Monitoring learning cost and regret

Finally, exploration policies in finance should be evaluated not only by eventual performance, but also by the *cost of learning*. Two useful concepts are:

- **Regret:** the cumulative difference between the reward obtained by the learning algorithm and the reward that would have been obtained by an oracle policy that knows the best action in hindsight.
- **Economic cost-of-learning:** the actual PnL shortfall, extra slippage, or increased risk incurred during the learning phase relative to a baseline policy.

By tracking regret and cost-of-learning over time, we can:

- compare exploration strategies (for example, ε-greedy vs. UCB vs. Thompson sampling in a bandit framework),
- decide when exploration should be reduced or stopped (when regret growth flattens and confidence in the learned policy is high),
- and communicate clearly to stakeholders how much "tuition" is being paid to acquire better strategies.

In this section, we moved from static problem formulation to the dynamic question of how an RL agent actually learns in markets:

- We emphasized that exploration in trading is costly and risky, requiring more structure than naive randomization.
- We introduced bandits and contextual bandits as simpler, data-efficient frameworks for problems like strategy and venue selection, where temporal effects can be abstracted away.
- We discussed structured exploration methods (UCB, Thompson sampling) and how they naturally incorporate uncertainty and context.
- We outlined safety-aware exploration techniques—constrained action spaces, gradual deployment, and uncertainty-aware decisions—to keep learning within acceptable risk boundaries.
- We highlighted the role of off-policy learning and historical data in reducing the need for live experimentation.

- Finally, we suggested guidelines for deciding when to upgrade from bandit formulations to full RL as temporal dependencies become central.

Together with the earlier sections on decision-process modeling, reward engineering, and state representation, these ideas complete the core toolkit for formulating and training reinforcement learning agents in financial markets. Subsequent chapters will build on this foundation to describe specific algorithms, simulation frameworks, and backtesting methodologies for deploying RL-based trading and execution strategies in practice.

Chapter 3

Algorithms and Data Infrastructure

In live markets, a clever idea is worthless if it cannot survive messy data and unforgiving execution. This chapter connects the theory of modern reinforcement learning-dynamic programming, value-based and policy-gradient methods, model-based and offline RL-with the practical infrastructure required to test them honestly: bias-aware data pipelines, realistic limit-order-book simulators, and tools to cope with shifting regimes. By the end, you will not only understand the algorithms, but also how to embed them in a research stack that produces strategies you can trust with real capital.

3.1 Dynamic Programming, Monte-Carlo, and Value-Based Deep RL

In earlier chapters we framed trading and portfolio problems as Markov decision processes (MDPs): at each decision time the agent observes a state summarizing market and portfolio information, chooses an action such as trading or rebalancing, receives a reward that reflects profit and risk, and transitions to a new state according to uncertain market dynamics.

This section develops the *value-function* view of such problems. Instead of directly searching over policies, we first ask a simpler question:

> Given that we are in a particular state and take a particular action, how good is that—on average and accounting for the future?

We formalize "how good" as a value function, show how dynamic programming (DP) solves small MDPs exactly, and then move step by step toward practical algorithms: Monte-Carlo (MC) policy evaluation, temporal-difference (TD) learning, Q-learning, and finally Deep Q-Networks (DQN) with extensions suited to discrete financial actions such as allocation buckets or execution slices.

The Value-Function View of Financial Decisions

Consider a discrete-time trading problem with decision times $t = 0, 1, 2, \ldots$. At each time:

- The *state* s_t includes variables such as current positions, recent returns, volatility estimates, bid–ask spreads, and possibly remaining time in an execution schedule.
- The *action* a_t represents a discrete trading decision: for example, one of five allocation buckets (strong underweight, slight underweight, neutral, slight overweight, strong overweight) in a portfolio context, or one of several execution slices (aggressive market order, passive limit order at best bid/ask, or no trade).
- The agent receives a scalar *reward* r_{t+1}, such as realized profit minus a penalty for risk, inventory, or transaction costs.

The long-term objective is to choose actions so as to maximize the expected cumulative discounted reward:

$$\mathbb{E}\left[\sum_{t=0}^{\infty} \gamma^t r_{t+1}\right],$$

where $0 < \gamma < 1$ is a discount factor that downweights distant rewards.

The central idea of value-based RL is to introduce value functions that quantify how attractive states and state–action pairs are, under a particular policy.

- The *state-value function* $V^\pi(s)$ is the expected discounted return starting in state s and following policy π thereafter.
- The *action-value function* $Q^\pi(s, a)$ is the expected discounted return starting in state s, taking action a once, and then following policy π.

An *optimal* value function V^* or Q^* corresponds to the best possible policy. If we knew Q^*, we could recover an optimal policy by choosing, in each state, the action that maximizes $Q^*(s, a)$.

In financial terms, you can think of $Q^\pi(s, a)$ as a generalized "risk-adjusted PnL forecast" for the action a given the current state s, where the forecast looks through time rather than just one step ahead. Estimating and improving these value functions is the central task of value-based RL.

Bellman Equations and Dynamic Programming

The value functions satisfy recursive relationships known as *Bellman equations*. Intuitively, the value of being in a state today equals the immediate payoff plus the discounted value of where you end up tomorrow.

For a given policy π, the Bellman equation for V^π is:

$$V^\pi(s) = \mathbb{E}\left[r_{t+1} + \gamma V^\pi(s_{t+1}) \mid s_t = s\right].$$

Similarly, the optimal state-value function V^* satisfies the *Bellman optimality equation*:

$$V^*(s) = \max_a \mathbb{E}\left[r_{t+1} + \gamma V^*(s_{t+1}) \mid s_t = s, a_t = a\right].$$

These equations say that if we knew V^* everywhere, we could determine the best action by taking the one whose combination of immediate reward and expected discounted continuation value is largest.

A toy financial MDP.

To make this concrete, imagine a very small execution problem over a short horizon. The state includes:

- Inventory bucket: {high inventory, low inventory}.
- Spread condition: {tight, wide}.
- Time step: $t = 0, 1, 2$ (finite horizon of three decisions).

The actions are {aggressive sell, passive sell, hold}. Immediate rewards combine execution price, spread, and a penalty for ending the episode with leftover inventory. Transition probabilities reflect simple rules of thumb: aggressive selling reduces inventory more quickly but may widen the spread; passive selling is cheaper but execution is uncertain.

The total number of state–action pairs is small enough that we can enumerate them. In such a setting, we can use classical dynamic programming:

- *Policy evaluation*: given a fixed policy, repeatedly apply the Bellman equation to compute its exact value function.
- *Policy improvement*: given the current value function, update the policy greedily to choose the best action in each state.
- *Policy iteration*: alternate evaluation and improvement steps until the policy stabilizes.
- *Value iteration*: repeatedly apply the Bellman optimality operator to update value estimates directly toward V^*.

In small, stylized market models, DP yields exact solutions. These models serve as intuition-building laboratories: they illustrate how future inventory and price impact should influence today's order choice. However, DP in this tabular form requires knowing the transition probabilities and rewards for all state–action pairs and becomes infeasible as the state space grows beyond a few dozen or hundred states.

From Planning to Learning: Monte-Carlo Evaluation

In realistic markets we rarely know the transition probabilities exactly; we can only observe trajectories of states, actions, and rewards. This moves us from *planning* (solving a known MDP by DP) to *learning* (estimating value functions from sample paths).

Monte-Carlo policy evaluation is the most direct way to learn from experience. Under a fixed policy π:

- Run many episodes (for example, simulate or backtest many execution days or rebalancing periods).
- For each visited state (or state–action pair), record the *return*: the discounted sum of rewards from that time until the end of the episode.
- Estimate the value of each state or state–action by averaging those returns over all episodes where it appeared.

In an execution context, one episode might represent the life of a parent order that must be executed within a given time window. The return could be defined as the negative implementation shortfall (so higher is better), possibly penalized for inventory risk. Monte-Carlo evaluation then estimates, for each state such as "half of the order filled, five minutes remaining, spread currently wide," the average quality of outcome if we continue using the current execution policy.

Monte-Carlo methods have two important properties:

- They do not require knowledge of transition dynamics; they rely entirely on sampled episodes.
- They only update value estimates at the end of episodes. This can be sample-inefficient for long horizons such as multi-month portfolio strategies.

The second point motivates temporal-difference methods, which update values more frequently by *bootstrapping* from existing estimates.

Temporal-Difference Learning and the Bias–Variance Trade-Off

Temporal-difference (TD) learning blends Monte-Carlo ideas with dynamic programming. Instead of waiting until the end of an episode to compute the full return, TD methods update value estimates using a one-step lookahead combined with the current estimate of the value of the next state.

For a state-value function, the simplest TD method (often called TD(0)) updates the estimate $V(s_t)$ toward the target

$$r_{t+1} + \gamma V(s_{t+1}).$$

For an action-value function, we analogously update $Q(s_t, a_t)$ toward

$$r_{t+1} + \gamma Q(s_{t+1}, a_{t+1}).$$

In financial terms, TD learning says: "After taking an action and seeing the next state and immediate reward, adjust your previous estimate of how good that state or state–action was by partially correcting it toward the observed one-step payoff plus the estimated continuation value."

Compared with Monte-Carlo:

- TD methods can learn online and incrementally, updating after each step rather than waiting until the end of the episode.
- TD targets involve the current value estimates, so they introduce some bias but reduce variance compared with full-return Monte-Carlo estimates.

This is a classic bias–variance trade-off. In long-horizon trading or portfolio problems, variance from full-episode returns can be enormous, because many distant random events influence the final outcome. Bootstrapping in TD methods tends to be more sample-efficient, which is crucial when historical data or high-fidelity simulation is expensive.

Q-Learning: Learning Optimal Policies from Experience

So far we have focused on evaluating a *given* policy. In practice, we usually want to *improve* policies toward optimality. Q-learning is a temporal-difference control method that directly seeks the optimal action-value function Q^* without requiring a separate policy improvement loop with explicit dynamics.

The Q-learning update for a visited state–action pair (s_t, a_t) is based on the TD target

$$r_{t+1} + \gamma \max_{a'} Q(s_{t+1}, a').$$

Intuitively, after taking an action and observing the next state and reward, we revise our estimate of $Q(s_t, a_t)$ in the direction of the best achievable value from the next state, according to our current estimates. The greedy "max over a'" in the target pulls the value function toward optimality.

In financial terms, $Q(s_t, a_t)$ approximates the long-term value of making decision a_t in state s_t—for example:

- In a bucketed allocation problem, $Q(s_t, a_t)$ might represent the expected risk-adjusted return from moving the portfolio to allocation bucket a_t given current factors, transaction costs, and constraints.
- In a discrete execution problem, $Q(s_t, a_t)$ might represent the expected cost (negative reward) of choosing a particular execution slice (for example, "sell 5% of remaining inventory aggressively now") given the current order book and remaining horizon.

In its tabular form, Q-learning maintains a table $Q(s, a)$ and updates entries as experience is observed. As with DP, this is only viable for MDPs with relatively small, discrete state and action spaces. Realistic financial states are high-dimensional and continuous. To scale to such settings we need function approximation, and in particular deep neural networks.

From Tables to Networks: Deep Q-Learning

Deep Q-Learning replaces the Q-table with a neural network $Q_\theta(s,a)$ parameterized by weights θ. The input to the network is a representation of the state, such as recent price and volume observations, features summarizing volatility and liquidity, inventory levels, and remaining time. The output is a vector of Q-values, one component per discrete action.

Training proceeds by minimizing the squared error between current Q-values and TD targets derived from experience. However, naively combining Q-learning with deep networks tends to be unstable because:

- The data distribution is non-stationary: as the policy improves, it visits different states.
- The TD targets depend on the network's own predictions, creating feedback loops.

The Deep Q-Network (DQN) architecture introduces stabilizing mechanisms:

- **Experience replay**: Store past experience tuples $(s_t, a_t, r_{t+1}, s_{t+1})$ in a replay buffer. Sample mini-batches uniformly (or with prioritization) to decorrelate updates and reuse data efficiently.
- **Target network**: Maintain a separate, slowly updated copy of the Q-network to generate TD targets. This reduces harmful feedback from rapidly changing targets.
- **Reward clipping and normalization**: In some applications, clipping rewards to a bounded range improves numerical stability. In finance, careful normalization (for example, scaling by volatility or notional) often plays a similar role while preserving relative magnitudes.
- **Action masking**: Enforce feasibility by masking out illegal or infeasible actions at a given time, such as trades that would violate inventory or leverage limits. The network only outputs Q-values for actions that obey current constraints.

In a portfolio allocation example, the actions might be discrete allocation shifts relative to a benchmark. The state could contain factor exposures, risk forecasts, and current positions. The DQN learns a mapping from states to Q-values for each shift (for example, "increase risk by one bucket," "decrease risk by two buckets"), and the policy typically selects the action with the highest Q-value, possibly with some exploration.

In an execution setting, the actions could represent discrete execution slices for a parent order: how aggressively to trade and what order type to use in the next interval. The DQN would learn which slice trades off market impact, spread cost, and execution risk most favorably, given current order book features and remaining time.

Illustrative Flow: From Tabular MDP to DQN

The conceptual progression from dynamic programming to deep Q-learning can be summarized in a flow diagram that connects the main ideas: small tabular MDPs, Monte-Carlo and TD updates, and the extension to DQN with experience replay and target networks. Figure provides such a schematic, annotated with financial examples of states and actions.

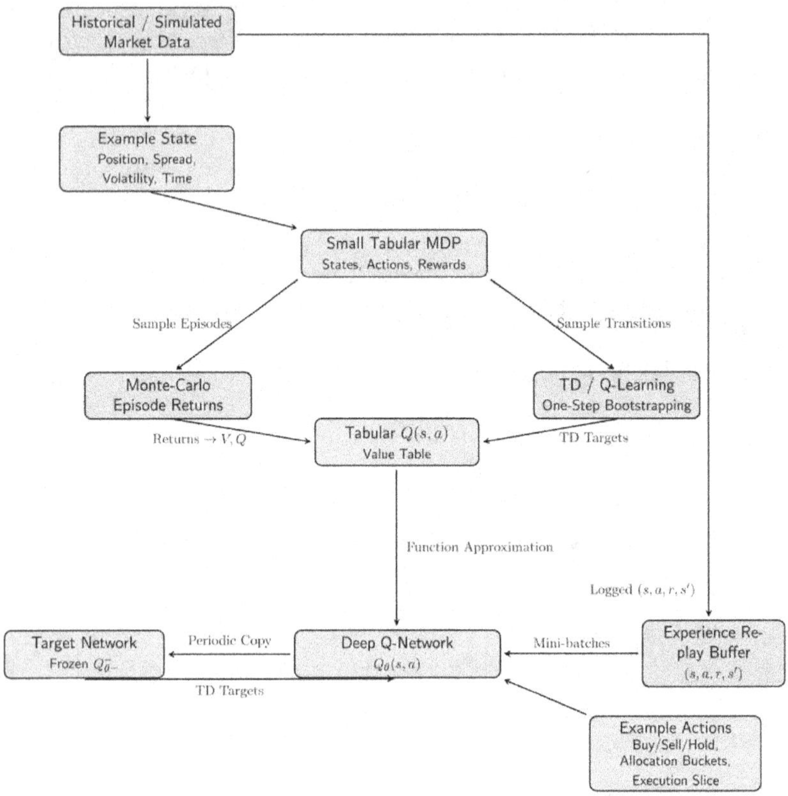

Distributional and Advanced Value-Based Methods

Once we have a basic DQN in place, several refinements become attractive in financial applications.

Double DQN. Standard DQN tends to overestimate Q-values because the same network both selects and evaluates the maximizing action in the TD target. Double DQN decouples these roles: one network selects the action (via arg max), while the target network evaluates it. This simple change often yields more conservative and accurate value estimates, which is especially important when exploiting small edges in noisy financial data.

Dueling DQN. Many states share similar overall "goodness," while differences mainly arise from which action is taken. Dueling architectures separate the estimation of a state-value baseline from the advantages of each action relative to that baseline. This can lead to more sample-efficient learning, particularly in markets where some aspects of the environment dominate the effect of specific actions.

Distributional RL. Traditional Q-learning focuses on the expected return. In finance, however, the shape of the return distribution matters: downside risk and tail events are crucial. Distributional RL methods approximate the full distribution of returns $Z(s, a)$ rather than just its mean. For example, they may model the value as a categorical distribution over a set of quantized return levels. Policies can then be optimized to account explicitly for risk preferences: minimizing the probability of large losses, controlling tail quantiles, or trading off mean and variance in a more nuanced way.

When to Use Value-Based Deep RL in Finance

Value-based deep RL, and DQN-style methods in particular, are well suited to problems with:

- **Discrete actions**: Allocation buckets, discrete position changes, execution slices, or order-type choices.
- **High-dimensional state**: Rich market microstructure signals, multi-asset features, and history windows encoded via convolutional or recurrent architectures.
- **Well-defined reward signals**: Execution cost, implementation shortfall, risk-adjusted PnL, or utility-based objectives over an episode or long horizon.

In such settings, learning a value function can be more stable and interpretable than directly optimizing a policy. The Q-values can be inspected and stress-tested under different market conditions, providing an additional layer of comfort before deployment.

In later sections we will complement this value-based perspective with policy-gradient and actor–critic methods, which are often more natural for continuous action spaces such as continuous portfolio weights or order sizes. However, many real-world trading and portfolio workflows are already organized around discrete decisions: bucketed risk limits, stepwise rebalancing, or discrete child-order slices in algorithmic execution. For those, the value-based deep RL toolkit developed here is both conceptually natural and practically powerful.

3.2 Policy Gradient and Actor-Critic Methods

In the previous section we approached trading and portfolio problems through *value functions*: we estimated $Q(s, a)$ or $V(s)$ and then chose actions by maximizing the learned values. This worked naturally for discrete actions such as allocation buckets or execution slices and led to Deep Q-Networks (DQN) and their variants.

Many important financial decisions, however, are more naturally expressed in *continuous* terms:

- Setting continuous portfolio weights across dozens of assets.
- Choosing the exact size and limit price of an order.
- Adjusting a volatility target or leverage multiplier on a sliding scale.

Extending value-based methods directly to continuous, high-dimensional actions is difficult. Maximizing $Q(s, a)$ over a continuous a can become intractable, and small changes in action can have subtle effects on risk and cost.

Policy-gradient and actor-critic methods address this challenge by learning a *policy function* directly. Instead of asking "what is the value of each action?" and then maximizing, we parameterize the action-selection rule itself and optimize it by gradient methods.

From Value Functions to Parameterized Policies

Recall the MDP structure: at each time t, the agent observes state s_t (market and portfolio features), chooses action a_t (for example, a vector of portfolio weights or an order size), receives reward r_{t+1}, and moves to a new state s_{t+1}.

A *policy* π is now represented by a parameterized function $\pi_\theta(a \mid s)$, where θ are the model parameters (for example, neural network weights). Given a state, π_θ outputs either:

- A probability distribution over discrete actions (for example, different order types), or
- A probability distribution over continuous actions (for example, a multivariate Gaussian over portfolio weights or order sizes).

Our goal is to adjust θ to maximize the expected discounted return. Policy-gradient methods provide a way to compute (or estimate) the gradient of performance with respect to θ, and then perform gradient ascent.

At a high level, the gradient tells us:

> Increase the probability of actions that led to higher returns, and decrease the probability of actions that led to lower returns.

This fits financial intuition: if a particular execution style tends to reduce implementation shortfall in certain market conditions, the policy should become more likely to choose that style in similar states.

Policy-Gradient Intuition in Financial Terms

To build intuition, consider an episodic execution problem. An episode is the life of a parent order that must be completed within a fixed time window. The state s_t includes:

- Remaining inventory fraction.

- Time remaining.
- Current spread, depth at best bid/ask, and short-term volatility.

The action a_t is a continuous number between 0 and 1 representing the fraction of remaining inventory to trade in the next interval (for instance, the next minute), combined with a choice of whether to use a market or limit order. The reward can be defined as negative execution cost (or negative slippage relative to a benchmark), possibly with a risk penalty for large unexecuted inventory late in the horizon.

A stochastic policy might, for each state, produce:

- A mean and standard deviation for the trade fraction (for example, higher mean and lower variance when we are behind schedule; lower mean but still some variance when we are ahead of schedule).
- A probability distribution over order types (for example, more likely to use passive orders in calm, liquid markets).

We run episodes using this policy, measure the realized returns (for instance, negative implementation shortfall), and then update the policy parameters so that actions that performed well in their contexts become more likely. Policy-gradient methods formalize this "credit assignment" from outcomes back to action probabilities.

Variance Reduction: Baselines and Advantages

Naively updating the policy by pushing up the probability of actions that happened in high-return episodes and pushing down probabilities in low-return episodes would be very noisy. In finance, noise is particularly severe: even a well-designed policy can have negative PnL in some episodes purely due to random market moves.

To obtain useful gradients, we must reduce variance. Two fundamental tools are:

Baselines. Instead of weighting actions by raw return, we weight them by (return minus a baseline). A common baseline is an estimate of the state value $V^\pi(s_t)$: how good we expect things to be from s_t under the current policy. This centers the gradient around zero: if the episode did better than usual from that state, we increase the probability of chosen actions; if it did worse than usual, we decrease it.

Advantages. The *advantage function* $A^\pi(s_t, a_t)$ measures how much better an action is compared with the policy's average action at that state:

$$A^\pi(s_t, a_t) = Q^\pi(s_t, a_t) - V^\pi(s_t).$$

In words, advantage answers: "Given that we are in state s_t, was taking action a_t better or worse than what we normally do?" Using advantages instead of raw returns further stabilizes learning, because it focuses updates on *relative* performance.

In execution, $A^\pi(s_t, a_t)$ could be positive when an unusually aggressive slice in a particular volatile interval reduced overall shortfall, and negative when the same aggressiveness caused unnecessary impact in a quiet market.

Actor-Critic Architectures

Baselines and advantages suggest that in addition to the policy (the "actor"), we should maintain a value estimator (the "critic") that predicts $V^\pi(s)$ or $Q^\pi(s, a)$.

An *actor-critic* method consists of:

- An **actor network** with parameters θ^{actor} that outputs a policy $\pi_{\theta^{actor}}(a \mid s)$.
- A **critic network** with parameters θ^{critic} that outputs a value estimate, often $V_{\theta^{critic}}(s)$.

The critic is trained by regression to minimize the error between its predicted value and a target based on observed rewards (for example, via TD learning). The actor is updated by a policy-gradient rule that uses the critic's outputs to form advantages or baselines.

In a multi-asset portfolio setting, the shared input to both networks might include:

- Factor returns and forecasts.
- Current portfolio weights.
- Risk model outputs (for example, predicted volatility and correlations).
- Transaction cost estimates.

The actor could output a mean vector of desired portfolio weight changes (possibly with a covariance structure for exploration), while the critic outputs an estimate of the risk-adjusted future return from the current state.

Actor-Critic Network Diagram

Figure shows a schematic actor-critic architecture tailored to trading applications. Market and portfolio features are passed through a shared encoder, then split into policy and value "heads." The critic produces value estimates, which are used both for TD updates and to form advantages that guide the actor's gradient updates.

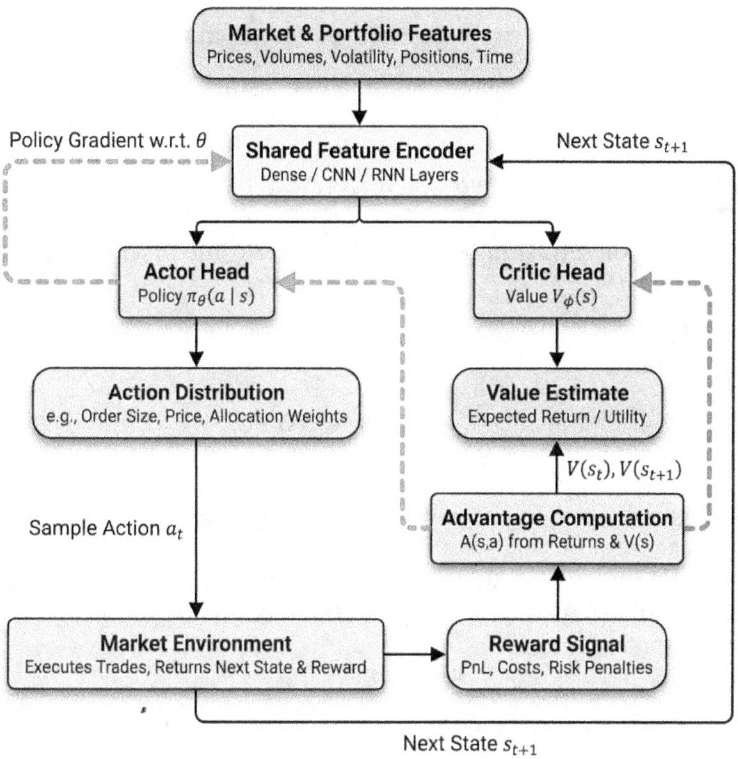

On-Policy Actor-Critic: A2C and A3C

A straightforward incarnation of actor-critic is the family of *on-policy* methods, such as Advantage Actor-Critic (A2C) and its asynchronous extension A3C. "On-policy" means that the same policy used to generate data is the one being updated.

The training loop typically alternates between:

1. Running the current policy for several steps (or an episode) in the environment, collecting (s_t, a_t, r_{t+1}).
2. Using the critic to form bootstrapped estimates of returns and

advantages (for example, by n-step TD methods).

3. Updating the critic parameters to better fit these targets.
4. Updating the actor parameters using the policy gradient weighted by the advantages.

In an episodic execution problem, A2C can be effective because:

- The horizon is finite and known (start time to completion deadline).
- The reward structure (implementation shortfall) is relatively well defined.
- Multiple independent episodes (orders) can be simulated or replayed in parallel.

A3C extends this idea by running multiple actor-critic workers in parallel, each interacting with its own copy of the environment and periodically updating a shared set of parameters. For computationally heavy trading simulators, this parallelization can dramatically increase throughput.

Generalized Advantage Estimation (GAE)

Even with a critic, estimating advantages can be noisy, especially for long-horizon problems such as dynamic asset allocation. If we rely on very short-horizon TD targets, bias increases because we ignore far-future rewards. If we rely on full-episode returns, variance is high.

Generalized Advantage Estimation (GAE) strikes a compromise by forming a weighted average of k-step advantage estimators. It introduces a parameter (often denoted by λ) that smoothly interpolates between high-bias, low-variance (short k) and low-bias, high-variance (long k) regimes.

In plain language:

> GAE says: "Let's credit each action with a mix of short-term and longer-term feedback, placing more weight on

near-term TD errors but not completely ignoring distant outcomes."

In portfolio management, this is important because small allocation changes can have effects that unfold over many days or weeks. Purely one-step TD would miss these delayed consequences, while pure Monte-Carlo would be overwhelmed by market noise. GAE allows us to harness multi-step information without letting variance explode.

Encouraging Exploration with Entropy Regularization

Financial markets are nonstationary and complex; sticking too quickly to one narrow behavior can be dangerous. Policy-gradient methods often include an *entropy regularization* term in the objective to encourage exploration.

Policy entropy measures how spread out the action distribution is. High entropy corresponds to a more mixed strategy; low entropy corresponds to nearly deterministic choices.

By adding a small bonus term proportional to policy entropy, we nudge the actor to keep some diversity in its actions, especially early in training. In a limit-order-book execution policy, entropy regularization might encourage occasional use of order types that appear suboptimal in the early data, but that could reveal profitable behaviors under different microstructure conditions.

In portfolio allocation, entropy regularization can prevent the policy from prematurely over-concentrating in a few assets, instead maintaining diversification while it learns more about return dynamics and transaction costs.

Trust Regions and Clipped Objectives: TRPO and PPO

A practical challenge with policy-gradient updates is that large parameter changes can drastically alter the policy. In a financial setting, such "policy jumps" can violate risk limits or produce wildly different trading patterns from one retraining run to the next.

Trust Region Policy Optimization (TRPO) and Proximal Policy Optimization (PPO) address this by constraining each update to make the new policy not too far from the old one.

TRPO. TRPO imposes a constraint on how much the policy's probability distribution over actions can change in each state, often measured by the Kullback-Leibler (KL) divergence. It then solves an approximate constrained optimization problem: maximize the policy-gradient objective subject to a bound on the average KL divergence between old and new policies.

PPO. PPO simplifies this idea by introducing a *clipped* objective that penalizes updates that would cause the new policy's action probabilities to deviate too much from the old ones. It is much easier to implement and has become a standard baseline for continuous-control tasks.

In a trading context, these trust-region and clipping ideas have clear interpretations:

- They reduce the risk of "catastrophic" policy changes that might, for example, double typical trading volume or radically change intraday execution patterns after a single training iteration.
- They can be aligned with operational risk controls: one can select trust-region or clipping hyperparameters that roughly correspond to acceptable changes in trade volumes, inventory profiles, or risk exposures between policy versions.

When training an RL-based execution algorithm on simulated or historical data, PPO provides a pragmatic default: it is on-policy, relatively stable, and handles continuous action outputs (for example, order sizes or allocation deltas) naturally.

Deterministic Policy Gradients and DDPG

So far we have focused on stochastic policies, which output distributions over actions. For some finance problems, especially those involving high-dimensional continuous actions, it is attractive to use *deterministic* policies instead. A deterministic policy maps each state to a single action: $a = \mu_\theta(s)$.

Deterministic Policy Gradient (DPG) methods derive a way to compute gradients for such policies using an off-policy critic $Q^\mu(s, a)$. The Deep Deterministic Policy Gradient (DDPG) algorithm combines:

- An actor network $\mu_\theta(s)$ (deterministic policy).
- A critic network $Q_\phi(s, a)$.
- Experience replay and target networks, much like DQN, to stabilize learning.

During training, exploration is introduced by adding noise to the actor's output actions (for example, Gaussian or Ornstein-Uhlenbeck noise). The critic learns from these noisy experiences, and the actor is updated to maximize the critic's estimate $Q_\phi(s, \mu_\theta(s))$.

DDPG is particularly natural for:

- **Continuous allocation problems** where the action is a vector of portfolio weights or weight changes across many assets.
- **Continuous sizing and pricing decisions** in execution, such as choosing precise order sizes and limit prices within allowed ranges.

Action bounding is essential: the actor output is typically passed through squashing functions and then rescaled to respect budget, leverage, or inventory constraints. For instance, the actor might output an unconstrained vector that is then normalized to sum to one (for a fully invested portfolio) and clipped to respect individual asset limits.

Choosing Between Value-Based and Policy-Gradient Methods

By this point, we have two broad families of RL techniques:

- **Value-based methods** (Q-learning, DQN, distributional DQN, etc.), which are powerful for discrete actions and can be data-efficient, but struggle with large continuous action spaces.

- **Policy-gradient and actor-critic methods** (A2C/A3C, PPO, DDPG, and others), which handle continuous, high-dimensional actions more naturally and provide smoother control over risk-related behavior, at the cost of higher variance in gradient estimates.

In practice:

- Use value-based deep RL when your decision space is inherently discrete (for example, bucketing, routing among a small set of execution strategies, on/off risk toggles).

- Use policy-gradient or actor-critic methods when your key levers are continuous (for example, allocation vectors, order sizes, pricing offsets, dynamic volatility targets), or when you need fine-grained control over the distribution of outcomes rather than just the expected return.

The remainder of this book will often combine these perspectives. For example, we may use an actor-critic framework with a critic that benefits from ideas in distributional RL, or we may discretize certain dimensions to leverage DQN-style methods while keeping others continuous under a policy-gradient approach.

In all cases, the core message of this section is that policy-gradient and actor-critic methods give us a principled way to optimize complex, continuous trading and execution policies, provided we invest in good value estimators (critics), advantage estimation, and stability mechanisms such as entropy regularization, trust regions, and clipped objectives.

3.3 Model-Based, Offline, and Safe/Constrained RL

The previous sections developed powerful online learning tools: value-based deep RL for discrete actions and policy-gradient/actor-critic methods for continuous, high-dimensional controls. All of these methods rely, at least in part, on *exploration* in the environment: the agent must try different actions to discover better strategies.

In financial markets, naive exploration is unacceptable. A policy that "tries things out" with real capital can easily violate risk limits, incur large losses, or breach regulatory constraints. Bridging the gap between flexible RL algorithms and strict real-world risk management requires three complementary ideas:

- **Model-based RL**: learn an approximate model of market dynamics and use it to plan or augment experience.
- **Offline (batch) RL**: learn policies from historical or simulated data without further exploration.
- **Safe and constrained RL**: incorporate explicit capital, drawdown, and turnover limits into the objective and learning procedure.

This section explains each idea in turn, and then describes how they can be combined into a practical workflow for deploying RL in live trading and portfolio management.

Why Model-Based, Offline, and Safe RL Matter in Finance

Before diving into details, it is useful to highlight what makes finance different from many benchmark RL domains:

- **Risk of rare but severe losses**: Catastrophic losses may occur infrequently, but are unacceptable to investors and regulators. An RL agent must be conservative about tail risk, not just maximize expected return.

- **Limited ability to explore**: You cannot simply "try random actions" with actual capital. Even paper trading or shadow strategies are constrained by compliance and operational limits.
- **Nonstationary and partially observable markets**: The environment changes over time, and many drivers of price and liquidity are not directly observable. Overfitting to one regime is dangerous.

Model-based, offline, and constrained RL techniques help by reducing dependence on risky online interaction, by structuring learning around logged data, and by embedding domain constraints directly into the optimization process.

Model-Based RL: Learning Market Dynamics for Planning

In model-based RL, we first approximate the environment's transition dynamics using a learned model, and then use this model for planning, simulation, or augmenting experience.

Formally, instead of treating the environment as a black box, we learn an approximate transition function

$$\hat{p}(s_{t+1}, r_{t+1} \mid s_t, a_t),$$

which predicts the next state and reward distribution from the current state and action. In finance, this model typically captures:

- Short-horizon price changes or returns.
- Spread and depth dynamics in the limit order book.
- Execution probabilities for different order types and sizes.
- Inventory evolution and transaction costs.

Sources of training data. The model is learned from:

- Historical trade and quote data (TAQ), filled and unfilled orders, and derived microstructure features.

- Backtest logs from existing execution algorithms or portfolio strategies.
- Synthetic data from stylized stochastic models calibrated to historical behavior.

Because the model is trained off-line on logged data, it can be improved over time without taking new live risk.

Using the model for planning.

Once a transition model is available, it can be used in several ways:

- **Pure planning:** Given a candidate policy, simulate many episodes under the model to estimate its performance and risk profile. For example, test how an execution policy behaves under a range of volatility and liquidity scenarios.
- **Model-predictive control (MPC):** At each decision time, simulate a finite look-ahead horizon under the model for various action sequences, and choose the first action of the best sequence. Re-plan at the next step using updated state information.
- **Dyna-style model-based RL:** Use the model to generate *imaginary* transitions (s, a, r, s') that augment real experience in training value functions or policies. This can improve sample efficiency.

In trading, MPC is particularly appealing for short-horizon tasks such as intraday execution or market making. The model can simulate microstructure responses to different order schedules, and the controller chooses the near-term action that looks best under those simulations, while re-optimizing as new information arrives.

Model bias and compounding error.

Model-based approaches introduce new risks: if the learned dynamics do not match the real environment, planning may produce systematically flawed strategies. Two key issues are:

- **Model bias**: The model is only an approximation; it may miss rare events (for example, flash crashes) or structural breaks.

- **Compounding error**: Small prediction errors can accumulate over long simulated horizons, making long-horizon forecasts unreliable.

Practical safeguards include:

- Calibrating the model on multiple regimes and stressing it on extreme scenarios.
- Limiting planning horizons to time scales where model predictions are reasonably accurate.
- Combining model-based rollouts with real-world data (Dyna-style) so that learning remains anchored in observed behavior.

Offline RL: Learning from Logged Financial Data

Offline (or batch) RL takes the opposite extreme: instead of learning from an interactive environment, we are given a fixed dataset of transitions collected under some *behavior policy* and must learn a new policy without further interaction.

In finance, this setting is natural and common. Firms often have:

- Large archives of historical execution logs, containing states (market and order book conditions), actions (orders sent), and outcomes (fills, prices, costs).
- Historical records of portfolio holdings and trades by human or rule-based strategies.

The challenge is that the dataset only covers the state-action pairs that the behavior policy visited. If a new policy proposes drastically different actions in some states, we may have little or no data on what would happen, leading to dangerous *extrapolation*.

Key concepts in offline RL.

Several ideas are essential to understanding offline RL in finance:

- **Dataset coverage:** How well does the logged data cover the state-action space that the new policy wants to explore? For example, if historical execution strategies were always conservative, the dataset may lack examples of very aggressive orders in illiquid periods. A policy that recommends such aggressive actions would be unsupported by data.

- **Extrapolation error:** Learning algorithms that freely generalize to unseen state-action regions can assign overly optimistic values there, leading the policy to choose actions with artificially high estimated returns but unknown actual risk.

- **Conservative value estimation:** To avoid extrapolation, offline RL methods often *underestimate* values in poorly supported regions, steering the learned policy closer to the behavior policy in those areas.

Behavior regularization and policy constraints.

A practical way to keep offline policies safe is to constrain them to stay close to the behavior policy where data is sparse. Techniques include:

- **Behavior cloning as a baseline:** First train a supervised model to mimic the behavior policy. This gives a reference policy that is guaranteed to stay within historically observed behavior.

- **Policy regularization:** When optimizing the new policy, add a penalty for deviating too far from the behavior policy (for example, a KL divergence penalty). This discourages radical departures unless the value estimates are strongly supported by data.

- **Action constraints:** Explicitly limit the range of actions, such as maximum order size or leverage, to levels that are common in the dataset.

In execution, an offline RL algorithm might learn from years of order logs to propose slightly more aggressive schedules in certain conditions, but only within a band around what has been historically observed. In portfolio allocation, offline RL can learn to adjust factor tilts or turnover in ways that fit within established trading styles and limits.

Offline evaluation.

Evaluating a new policy offline is non-trivial, because we cannot observe its actions' outcomes directly. Common tools include:

- **Off-policy evaluation**: Statistical estimators (for example, importance sampling, doubly robust estimators) that reweight logged trajectories to approximate how the new policy would have performed. These can be high variance but are useful as rough diagnostics.
- **Replay in simulators**: Use a high-fidelity market simulator calibrated to historical data to test the new policy before any live deployment.

Robust offline evaluation is a precondition for safely moving RL strategies into even small-scale live trials.

Safe and Constrained RL: Capital, Drawdown, and Turnover Limits

Thus far we have focused on maximizing expected return (or minimizing cost) under an implicit assumption of risk-aversion encoded via reward shaping. In institutional finance, however, there are explicit constraints:

- Maximum allowed leverage or capital usage.
- Limits on single-name or sector exposures.
- Maximum drawdown thresholds over certain horizons.
- Turnover budgets due to transaction costs and market impact.
- Regulatory and mandate-specific rules (for example, concentration limits, short-selling restrictions).

Safe and constrained RL provides formal tools to incorporate such limits into the decision-making process.

Constrained Markov decision processes (CMDPs).

A constrained MDP extends the standard RL formulation with additional *cost signals* and bounds. Besides reward r_{t+1}, we define cost components $c^1_{t+1}, c^2_{t+1}, \dots$ representing, for example:

- Capital usage (for leverage).
- Incremental turnover.
- Realized drawdown contribution.

We seek a policy that maximizes expected reward subject to constraints on the cumulative discounted (or average) costs, such as:

$$\mathbb{E}[C^k(\pi)] \le d_k \quad \text{for each constraint } k.$$

Conceptually, the agent must respect budget-like limits on capital, drawdown, or turnover while still seeking high reward.

Lagrangian and primal-dual methods.

One principled way to solve CMDPs is to introduce Lagrange multipliers λ_k for each constraint, forming a combined objective:

$$\mathbb{E}\left[\sum_t \gamma^t \left(r_{t+1} - \sum_k \lambda_k c^k_{t+1}\right)\right] + \sum_k \lambda_k d_k.$$

In words, we transform the constrained problem into an unconstrained one with a *penalized reward*:

$$r^{\text{penalized}}_{t+1} = r_{t+1} - \sum_k \lambda_k c^k_{t+1}.$$

The multipliers λ_k are adjusted over time:

- If a constraint is violated (for example, average turnover exceeds its budget), increase λ_k to penalize that cost more heavily.
- If a constraint is slack (for example, capital usage is far below the limit), decrease λ_k to allow more flexibility.

We can apply policy-gradient or actor-critic methods to the penalized reward while simultaneously updating λ_k via gradient ascent on the Lagrangian. This *primal-dual* approach encourages convergence to policies that satisfy the constraints on average.

In portfolio management, one might define c^1_{t+1} as a measure of realized risk (for example, squared portfolio return) and c^2_{t+1} as turnover. The Lagrangian method trades off performance against these costs in a controlled, adaptive manner.

Practical safety layers.

Beyond formal CMDP approaches, practitioners often apply simpler but robust safety measures:

- **Action clipping and projection:** Force the RL agent's suggested actions to respect hard constraints by clipping (for example, cap order sizes, enforce maximum leverage) or projecting onto a feasible set (for example, re-normalize portfolio weights to obey exposure constraints).
- **Risk filters:** Wrap the learned policy inside a rule-based risk engine that can veto or scale down actions when risk metrics (for example, VaR, stress losses, liquidity measures) exceed thresholds.
- **Fallback policies:** Maintain a conservative baseline policy (for example, a benchmark execution schedule or strategic asset allocation) and allow the RL policy to deviate only within controlled bands. If performance or risk metrics degrade, revert to the baseline.

These heuristics may not be mathematically optimal, but they embody institutional risk culture and provide an additional line of defense against model errors and regime shifts.

Combining Model-Based, Offline, and Safe RL in Practice

In real trading organizations, robust RL workflows typically combine the ideas above rather than relying on any single technique. A pragmatic development pipeline might look like this:

- **Data collection and environment modeling.** Build high-quality datasets of market states, actions, and outcomes from historical logs. Fit models of short-horizon dynamics (prices, spreads, execution probabilities) that can serve both as simulators and as components in risk models.

- **Offline policy learning.** Using the logged data (and possibly synthetic data from models), train initial policies with offline RL methods. Employ behavior regularization and action constraints to keep learned policies close to historically safe behaviors.

- **Risk-aware objective design.** Define rewards and cost signals that reflect the institution's real objectives: risk-adjusted return, capital usage, drawdown, turnover, and regulatory compliance. Decide which quantities should be hard constraints and which should be soft penalties.

- **Constrained fine-tuning in simulation.** In a high-fidelity simulator calibrated to real data, fine-tune policies using model-based or on-policy RL with explicit constraints (for example, via Lagrangian methods) and safety layers (clipping, risk filters).

- **Offline evaluation and stress testing.** Evaluate candidate policies offline using off-policy evaluation, replay in simulators, and structured stress tests (for example, crisis periods, liquidity droughts, volatility spikes). Reject policies that breach constraints under adverse scenarios.

- **Gradual online deployment.** Introduce the RL policy in a limited-capital, tightly monitored setting (for example, a small slice of total flow). Continue to log all data, monitor risk metrics in real time, and retain strong kill switches and fallback policies.

- **Continuous updating with guardrails.** As more data accumulates, periodically retrain or update models and policies using a mix of offline RL and cautious online learning. Constraints and safety filters are maintained and updated in parallel.

This workflow acknowledges that, in finance, the "environment" is not a toy simulator but the real market. Model-based, offline, and safe/constrained RL techniques allow us to exploit the flexibility of modern RL algorithms while staying within the boundaries set by capital preservation, regulatory rules, and client mandates.

Model-based RL uses learned market dynamics to plan and to augment scarce real data. Offline RL learns from existing logs without new exploration, but must guard against extrapolation and over-optimistic value estimates. Safe and constrained RL treats capital, drawdown, and turnover limits as first-class citizens, embedded either through formal constrained optimization or through robust safety layers around the learned policy.

Together, these approaches form the foundation for moving reinforcement learning from backtests and simulators into production-grade trading and portfolio systems. In the following section, we turn to the data engineering and simulation infrastructure needed to implement these ideas reliably and reproducibly.

3.4 Market Data Engineering and Simulation Environments

The previous sections have focused on algorithms: how to represent policies and value functions, how to incorporate constraints, and how to stabilize learning. All of these methods, however, are only as sound as the data and environments on which they are trained and evaluated. In finance this dependency is particularly acute. Microstructure noise, missing ticks, stale quotes, corporate actions, and regime shifts can easily distort signals and invalidate conclusions if not handled carefully.

This section presents the data and environment side of reinforcement learning for trading and portfolio management. We will:

- Outline the stages of a robust market data pipeline, from raw feeds to an RL-ready dataset.
- Discuss how to clean, align, and enrich heterogeneous data sources.

- Describe the design of realistic limit-order-book (LOB) and portfolio simulators that expose RL-style interfaces.
- Address nonstationarity and regime shifts, and how to structure experiments to remain robust under changing market conditions.
- Emphasize reproducibility and experiment management, so that results can be trusted and extended over time.

Why Data Engineering Matters for RL in Finance

In many standard RL benchmarks (for example, board games or robotic simulators), the environment is perfectly specified and noise-free by construction. In contrast, real-world financial data is:

- **Noisy**: Trades and quotes may contain outliers, misprints, or latency artifacts.
- **Heterogeneous**: Multiple venues, asset classes, and data vendors produce feeds at different granularities and with different conventions.
- **Evolving**: Market rules, tick sizes, and typical liquidity conditions change over time.

For RL, where the agent interacts with an environment and continually updates its policy, poor data engineering can lead not only to biased backtests but also to unstable learning and misleading policy updates. A robust pipeline and simulation environment is therefore the foundation on which all subsequent algorithmic sophistication rests.

From Raw Feeds to RL-Ready Data: An End-to-End Pipeline

Figure summarizes the main stages of a typical data pipeline for RL in trading: ingestion of raw market feeds, data cleaning and alignment, feature engineering, construction of an RL-ready dataset, and finally feeding that dataset into a simulator that interacts with an RL agent.

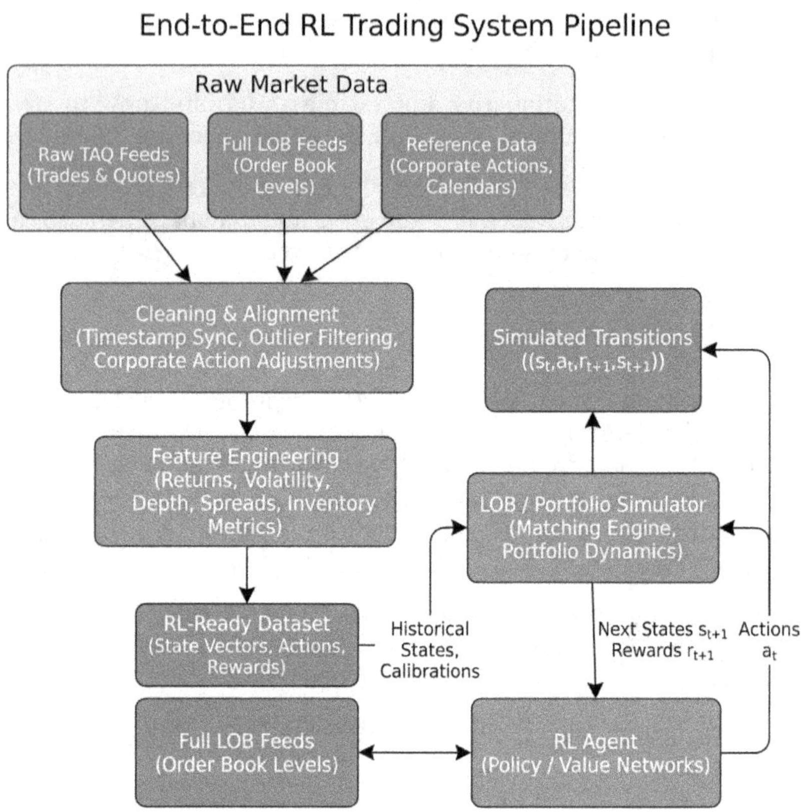

We now walk through each stage in more detail.

Market Data Sources and Ingestion

RL for trading typically relies on several categories of input data:

- **Trades and quotes (TAQ):** Time-stamped trades, best bid and ask quotes, and top-of-book sizes. This forms the backbone for mid-price, spread, and basic liquidity measures.
- **Full-depth limit-order-book feeds:** Snapshots or event streams of multiple price levels, with order additions,

modifications, and cancellations. These are essential for detailed execution and market-making tasks.

- **Reference and corporate action data:** Splits, dividends, symbol changes, trading halts, and calendars (for example, holidays, early closes). Without correct adjustments, historical prices and volumes are misleading.
- **Portfolio and execution logs:** Historical positions, trades, and realized PnL from existing strategies. These logs are vital for offline RL and for calibrating simulators to realistic behavior.

Ingestion involves connecting to vendor feeds or internal data stores, validating schemas and field types, and organizing raw data into a storage layout that supports efficient retrieval (for example, partitioned by date, symbol, and venue). At this stage the goal is fidelity: preserve as much of the original information as possible while ensuring basic integrity (no corrupted records, correct parsing of timestamps and prices).

Cleaning, Alignment, and Corporate Actions

Raw market data is messy. Before we can present it as a coherent environment to an RL agent, we must clean and align it.

Timestamp alignment. Different feeds (for example, trades and quotes from multiple venues) may have inconsistent timestamps due to latency and clock differences. A common approach is to:

- Convert all timestamps to a standardized timezone and format.
- Align events to a regular grid (for example, 100 ms or 1 s bars) by aggregating or interpolating.
- Ensure that, at each decision time step in the RL environment, the state reflects all information that would have been available at that time (no look-ahead).

In a multi-venue execution setting, the state might include consolidated best bid/ask across venues and venue-specific depths, all aligned to the agent's decision clock.

Handling missing data and outliers. Real feeds contain gaps and errors: missing intervals, zero or negative prices, abnormally large volumes or spreads. Simple but systematic rules help:

- Mark and possibly drop intervals where the feed is clearly broken (for example, entire seconds with obviously stale quotes).
- Winsorize or filter extreme values that violate basic plausibility (for example, price jumps of thousands of percent between adjacent ticks) unless justified by corporate events.
- Forward-fill or interpolate within short gaps when appropriate, being careful not to smear sharp events that matter for execution.

For RL tasks, it is often safer to exclude problematic intervals or days entirely from training rather than risk contaminating the environment with artifacts.

Adjusting for corporate actions. For equities and related instruments, corporate actions such as splits, dividends, and rights issues need to be handled consistently. Two typical strategies are:

- **Back-adjusted prices and volumes:** Construct a continuous series in which historical data is adjusted so that price paths are smooth across events.
- **Explicit corporate event modeling:** Keep raw prices but include event flags in the state and adjust PnL calculations appropriately.

For many RL applications, back-adjusted series are simpler and reduce spurious signals around event dates. However, execution simulators must still respect the actual trading rules and tick sizes that prevailed at the time.

Feature Engineering for RL States and Rewards

Once data is cleaned and aligned, we transform it into state vectors and reward signals appropriate for RL.

Price and return features. Rather than using raw prices, states often include:

- Log returns over multiple horizons (for example, 1 s, 10 s, 1 min).
- Moving averages or trend indicators.
- Volatility estimators: rolling standard deviations or realized volatility metrics.

These features help the agent recognize patterns like trending vs. mean-reverting behavior or volatility regimes.

Liquidity and microstructure features. For execution and market-making tasks, the state should reflect the local liquidity landscape:

- Current bid and ask prices and sizes; depth at several levels.
- Spread and its recent history.
- Order flow imbalance: net buying vs. selling pressure.
- Queue position and own outstanding orders in the book, if modeled.

Incorporating these features allows the agent to condition its policy on whether the market is tight and deep or wide and thin.

Portfolio and risk features. For allocation problems, states include:

- Current portfolio weights or positions.
- Factor exposures and risk model outputs.
- Turnover history and realized transaction costs.
- Risk limits or capital usage as state variables, so that the agent can anticipate upcoming constraints.

Rewards must also be engineered carefully. For example, immediate rewards might combine short-horizon PnL with penalties for risk, inventory, or impact, while terminal rewards capture long-horizon objectives such as final execution cost or end-of-day portfolio value.

Designing Limit-Order-Book and Portfolio Simulators

With an RL-ready dataset in hand, we can construct simulators that expose a standard RL interface: at each time step, the agent observes a state, chooses an action, and the simulator returns a reward and next state.

Event-Driven LOB Simulators

A high-fidelity LOB simulator aims to reproduce how the exchange's matching engine would respond to the agent's orders, given an underlying stream of background market events.

Key components include:

- **Background order flow:** Either replayed from historical messages or generated by a stochastic model calibrated to real data (for example, Poisson or Hawkes processes for limit and market order arrivals).
- **Matching logic:** A matching engine that maintains the book, processes incoming orders, and updates trades and quotes according to actual exchange rules (price-time priority, partial fills, cancellations).
- **Agent order handling:** The agent can submit market orders, limit orders at various price levels, or cancellations. The simulator updates the agent's inventory, cash, and outstanding orders accordingly.

This level of detail is crucial when training RL policies for intraday execution, market making, or optimal placement strategies. For example, the reward may depend on fill prices and quantities, while the state evolves based on both market events and the agent's actions.

Because full-depth LOB simulation is computationally intensive, many implementations use a hybrid approach:

- For extremely detailed studies, replay full historical message data with the agent's orders inserted.

- For larger-scale RL training, use a simplified stochastic model that approximates key behaviors (spread dynamics, impact, fill probabilities) while maintaining computational efficiency.

Portfolio Simulators

For multi-asset portfolio problems, the simulator typically operates on bar data (for example, daily or intraday bars) rather than tick data. A portfolio simulator performs:

- **State updates:** Given current holdings, prices, and risk factors, compute PnL, risk metrics, and updated state variables.
- **Trade execution model:** Apply a cost model to orders generated by the policy, including bid-ask spreads, market impact, and possibly delay.
- **Constraint enforcement:** Ensure that positions obey leverage, concentration, and other mandate constraints. This may involve projecting actions onto a feasible set.

Here, an "episode" may represent a rebalancing horizon (for example, several months), and the reward at each step combines realized return with penalties for risk and turnover.

Handling Nonstationarity and Regime Shifts

Financial markets are not stationary. Volatility regimes, correlation structures, liquidity conditions, and microstructure features can all change over time. Training an RL agent on one period and deploying it unchanged in another can be dangerous.

Several strategies help manage nonstationarity:

Rolling and expanding windows. Instead of training on all historical data at once, we can:

- Use rolling windows: train on a recent window (for example, the past two years), validate on the following months, and update the window forward over time.

- Use expanding windows with time decay: give higher weight to more recent data in loss functions or sampling.

This focuses learning on regimes that are more relevant to current conditions.

Regime detection and clustering. We can attempt to identify distinct market regimes, such as:

- Low-volatility vs. high-volatility periods.
- Normal vs. stressed liquidity conditions.
- Trend-dominated vs. mean-reverting environments.

Simple regime detection may rely on thresholds for realized volatility, spreads, or volume, while more sophisticated approaches cluster high-dimensional feature vectors. We can then:

- Train separate policies or simulators for different regimes.
- Condition a single policy on a regime indicator included in the state.
- Maintain a library of environment configurations, each calibrated to a particular regime, and randomize over them during training.

Domain randomization and stress testing. To improve robustness, simulators can randomize certain parameters (for example, average spreads, impact coefficients, volatility levels) within plausible ranges during training. This prevents the policy from overfitting to a single historical configuration and better prepares it for unseen conditions.

Additionally, explicit stress tests in extreme scenarios (for example, crisis periods or simulated jumps) are crucial to understand failure modes before deployment.

Reproducibility and Experiment Management

Robust data and simulation infrastructure should support not only accurate environments but also reproducible experiments. In RL, where stochasticity arises from initial conditions, action sampling, and environment noise, reproducibility is non-trivial but essential.

Key practices include:

- **Versioning data:** Keep immutable snapshots of the cleaned and feature-engineered datasets used for each experiment. When corporate action or cleaning logic changes, create new versions rather than overwriting old ones.
- **Versioning simulators:** Tag simulator code and configuration (for example, impact models, matching logic, randomization ranges) with explicit versions tied to experiment results.
- **Random seed management:** Record random seeds for policy initialization, action sampling, and environment noise for each run, so that behaviors can be replicated as closely as possible.
- **Config and hyperparameter logging:** Store all relevant settings (learning rates, network architectures, reward definitions, constraint parameters) alongside performance metrics and diagnostics.

Within a trading organization, these practices are not just academic niceties; they underpin model risk management, regulatory scrutiny, and the ability to debug unexpected live behavior.

Putting It All Together

Market data engineering and simulation environments form the backbone of reinforcement learning for finance. A typical workflow involves:

1. Ingesting and cleaning heterogeneous market and reference data.

2. Aligning and adjusting for corporate actions to produce coherent, high-quality time series.
3. Engineering state and reward features that capture price dynamics, liquidity, risk, and costs relevant to the decision problem.
4. Building simulators-both detailed LOB engines and higher-level portfolio models-that expose standard RL interfaces while respecting real-world frictions and constraints.
5. Accounting for nonstationarity through rolling windows, regime detection, and domain randomization.
6. Maintaining rigorous reproducibility through data and simulator versioning and careful experiment logging.

With these components in place, the algorithms introduced earlier in this chapter-dynamic programming, deep Q-learning, policy gradients, actor-critic, and constrained RL-can be applied with far greater confidence. The result is not only better backtest performance, but also a more reliable foundation for real-world deployment, where the true test of any RL system is its behavior under live, evolving market conditions.

Chapter 4

Reinforcement Learning for Dynamic Portfolio Management

Most portfolio models treat allocation as a static optimization problem. Real markets are anything but static. In this chapter we rebuild portfolio management as a sequential decision process and let reinforcement learning agents drive the wheel-learning when to rebalance, how hard to trade, and how to stay within tight risk and cost limits. You will see how to connect alpha signals, risk constraints, and execution frictions into a single, dynamic policy that can adapt as the market regime shifts.

4.1 Signal Integration and Feature Neutralization

In the previous chapter, we formulated portfolio management as a Markov decision process: at each decision time the agent observes a state, chooses an action that modifies the portfolio, and then receives a reward based on the resulting performance. From a reinforcement learning (RL) perspective, everything hinges on the quality of the *state*. If the state is noisy, unstable, or dominated by irrelevant risk exposures, even the best RL algorithm will struggle.

This section explains how to go from raw financial information—prices, volumes, fundamental data, macro indicators, and bespoke alpha signals—to a clean, factor-aware state representation suitable for an RL allocation agent. We will:

- Revisit style premia and alpha factors as building blocks.
- Define practical state variables for dynamic allocation.
- Show how to normalize and fuse heterogeneous signals.
- Introduce feature neutralization to remove unintended exposures.
- Discuss pitfalls such as lookahead bias and regime breaks.
- Give concrete examples of state designs for different portfolio types.

The main idea is that we want a state that is rich enough to capture the information content of our alphas, but clean enough that the agent does not simply rediscover trivial bets on broad risk factors (such as the market index or sector tilts) or overfit to artefacts of the data.

From Style Premia and Alphas to RL Signals

Most quantitative portfolio strategies start from the same basic ingredients:

- **Style premia:** systematic patterns such as value, momentum, quality, size, low volatility, and carry that historically earn a risk premium over long horizons.
- **Bespoke alpha signals:** more customized features, for example analyst revisions, earnings surprises, intraday order flow, options-implied skew, or macro news sentiment.

- **Risk factors:** exposures to market, sectors, countries, yield curve level and slope, credit, FX, and so forth, typically summarized via a factor model.

In a traditional factor model, these signals enter either as predictors of expected return (alpha factors) or as descriptors of common risk (risk factors). In an RL setting, we do not directly feed forecasts of return or risk into a static optimizer. Instead, we build an evolving *state* that the agent uses to decide how to reallocate the portfolio over time.

To make this concrete, imagine we trade a universe of N stocks daily. For each stock and each day, we may have:

- Past returns over various horizons (1-day, 5-day, 20-day).
- Fundamental ratios (book-to-price, earnings yield, leverage).
- Quality metrics (return on equity, gross margins).
- Volatility and liquidity measures (realized volatility, bid–ask spread).
- Cross-sectional factor exposures (market beta, sector dummies, size).

Naively concatenating everything into one huge vector and feeding it to a neural network rarely works well. Different variables live on different scales, update at different frequencies, and may be strongly collinear. Worse, many of these signals are simply different views of the same underlying broad risk factors. If we are not careful, the RL agent will "learn" easy but fragile strategies like "always be long high-beta tech when volatility is low," which may backtest beautifully but collapse under stress.

This motivates a structured transformation from raw inputs to a coherent RL state.

A Data-Flow View: From Raw Inputs to RL State

Before diving into the details, it is useful to visualize the data-processing pipeline that takes us from raw market data to a compact, neutralized state vector. This block diagram emphasizes that signal engineering for RL is a multi-stage process with clear responsibilities at each stage.

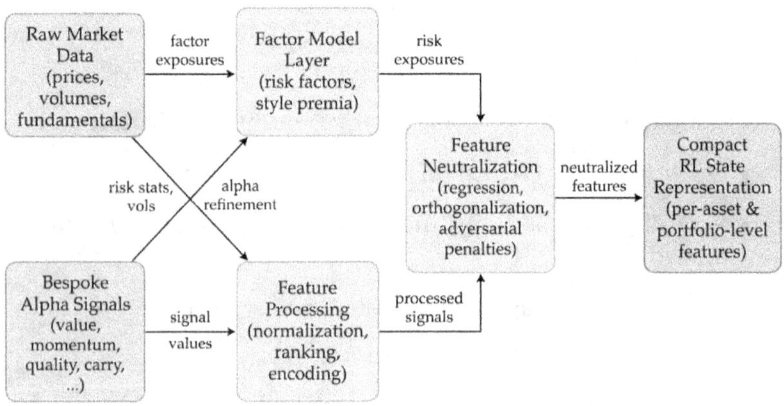

We will now unpack each of these stages and show how they contribute to a robust state representation.

Defining the RL State for Dynamic Allocation

An RL portfolio state normally has two main components:

1. **Per-asset features:** information about each security that we might trade.
2. **Portfolio-level features:** information summarizing the current portfolio and market regime.

Per-Asset Features

Per-asset features are where most factor and alpha signals live. Typical examples include:

- **Cross-sectional ranks of signals:** Instead of using raw price-to-book or momentum returns, we use their rank within the universe on that date, possibly scaled to lie between -1 and $+1$. This makes signals more robust to extreme values and easier to mix across assets and time.
- **Standardized factor exposures:** Betas to market, sectors, regions, size, and other risk factors, usually standardized to zero mean and unit variance across the universe.
- **Recent realized volatility and liquidity:** e.g., 20-day volatility, average daily dollar volume, bid–ask spread proxy.
- **Past returns over several horizons:** short (1–5 day), medium (1 month), and long (3–12 month) lookbacks.

For a universe of N assets, these features form a matrix with shape "number of assets by number of per-asset features" at each decision time.

Portfolio-Level Features

Portfolio-level features give context to the agent. They answer questions such as: How invested are we? How concentrated? Are we currently in a high-volatility regime?

Examples include:

- Current holdings: weights per asset, cash balance, gross exposure, net exposure.
- Aggregated risk exposures: portfolio beta to market, sector exposures, country exposures, duration, and so on.
- Performance summaries: recent portfolio returns, rolling Sharpe ratio, realized drawdown.
- Market regime indicators: index volatility, credit spreads, term spread, macro surprises.

Together, per-asset and portfolio-level features define the state s_t at time t.

Normalizing and Fusing Heterogeneous Signals

Because financial signals come from diverse sources and scales, normalization and fusion are essential before presenting them to an RL agent.

Time-Series Normalization

Many features benefit from time-series normalization, which reduces non-stationarity. For instance:

- Transform returns or ratios into z-scores using a rolling window per asset.
- Apply log transforms to strictly positive variables (like volume or market cap) to compress ranges.
- Cap extreme values at fixed quantiles or a small multiple of the rolling standard deviation.

The goal is to make each feature evolve in a relatively stable range so the agent does not have to constantly relearn what "large" or "small" means as the market drifts.

Cross-Sectional Ranking

For cross-sectional strategies, ranking assets by a signal at each time step is often more informative than using the raw value. A classic example is momentum: instead of the exact past-12-month return, we can use a rank between 0 and 1 (or rescaled to $[-1, 1]$). This has several benefits:

- Robustness to outliers and extreme values.
- Invariance to overall market level shifts.
- Easier mixing of different signals that naturally live on different scales.

Most factor-based equity RL agents use a mix of normalized raw features and cross-sectional ranks.

Neural Encoders for Per-Asset Features

Once we have a matrix of per-asset features, we can optionally use a neural encoder to produce compact embeddings. For example:

- A shallow feed-forward network that maps each asset's feature vector to a low-dimensional embedding.
- A graph or attention-based network that allows information sharing across assets based on sector or correlation structure.

The resulting embeddings can then be concatenated with portfolio-level features to form the final state. Importantly, these encoders should be designed and trained carefully to balance expressiveness and stability. Overly complex encoders may overfit to noise in the factor data, especially if the training window is limited.

Feature Neutralization: Removing Unintended Exposures

Even with careful normalization and encoding, factors and alpha signals often carry unintended exposures to broad risks like the market, sectors, value versus growth, or size. For instance, a naive momentum signal can be heavily tilted towards small-cap technology stocks during certain periods. If we feed this directly to an RL agent, it may "learn" that a particular sector or beta level is always good, simply because that happened to coincide with strong momentum in the training sample.

Feature neutralization aims to remove these unwanted components from the representation so that:

- The agent learns to exploit *true* stock-specific or diversified factor information.
- The policy is less sensitive to shifts in broad risk premia.
- Risk management becomes easier because exposures are explicit, not hidden inside black-box features.

We discuss three complementary approaches.

Cross-Sectional Regression (Pre-Processing Neutralization)

A simple and effective way to neutralize a signal with respect to known risk factors is to run a cross-sectional regression at each time step. Conceptually:

1. Choose risk factors to neutralize against (e.g., market beta, sector dummies, size, value).
2. For each date, regress your signal across assets on these factors.
3. Use the residuals of this regression as the neutralized signal.

Intuitively, you are explaining away any part of the signal that can be linearly attributed to broad factors. The remainder is orthogonal (in a least-squares sense) to those factors and thus less likely to simply reflect, say, "being long small caps."

This can be applied to many per-asset features:

- Neutralize momentum with respect to size and sector.
- Neutralize value with respect to country and industry.
- Neutralize combined alpha scores with respect to market beta and volatility.

The neutralized features then feed into your encoder and, ultimately, into the RL state.

Orthogonalization in Feature Space

When dealing with many highly correlated features, it is often helpful to orthogonalize them systematically. One intuitive procedure is:

- Order features by their perceived importance or robustness.
- For each feature in turn, regress it on all previously accepted features and replace it by the residual.

The resulting set is approximately orthogonal: each new feature contributes incremental information that is not linearly redundant with the existing ones. This serves two purposes:

- Reduces multicollinearity, which can destabilize both supervised models and RL algorithms.
- Makes it easier to interpret what the agent is learning, because features represent more distinct sources of variation.

Compared to simple scaling or PCA-like dimensionality reduction, orthogonalization can be guided by domain knowledge: we can choose to retain some anchor factors (e.g., robust value and momentum signals) and make others orthogonal to them.

Adversarial Penalties (Learned Neutralization)

In modern deep RL setups, we can go beyond static pre-processing and learn to neutralize features jointly with the RL policy. A powerful idea is to use an *adversarial* or *auxiliary* network that tries to recover factor exposures from the internal representation, while we train the representation to make this prediction difficult.

The general pattern is:

- The encoder maps raw per-asset inputs to an intermediate representation.
- An adversary network takes this representation and tries to predict undesired exposures (e.g., portfolio beta, sector weights).
- The training objective encourages the encoder to be good for the main RL task but bad for the adversary, effectively discouraging the encoding of unwanted factor information.

This approach is more flexible than fixed regression, but also more complex and data-hungry. It is particularly useful when undesired exposures are nonlinear or when the mapping from features to risk factors changes over time.

Practical Considerations and Pitfalls

Building a robust RL state is not only about clever transformations. Several practical issues can quietly undermine the entire setup if not addressed carefully.

Avoiding Data Leakage and Lookahead Bias

Data leakage occurs when the state at time t uses information that is not truly available at t in a live setting. Common examples include:

- Using end-of-day closing prices to compute intraday signals.
- Using revised or restated fundamentals instead of point-in-time values.
- Letting your factor model use future information implicitly (for example, through an in-sample covariance estimate that spans the whole backtest).

In RL this is particularly dangerous because the agent can implicitly exploit such leaks in highly nonlinear ways. To prevent this, enforce strict time alignment: every component of the state must be computable using only information that would have been available just before the decision time in historical data.

Choosing State Horizon and Refresh Frequency

The state may include short histories of certain features (e.g., last 5 days of volatility or returns). A longer history gives more context but increases dimensionality and the risk of overfitting. A practical compromise is:

- Use a small number of carefully chosen lookback windows (e.g., 5, 20, 60 days) rather than full time series.
- Refresh the state at the same frequency as decisions (e.g., daily or hourly).
- If using intraday data, consider summarizing it into a few statistics per day (high/low ranges, realized volatility) instead of raw tick data.

The right horizon is problem-dependent: high-frequency execution agents need granular, short-horizon states; strategic asset allocation agents can work with coarser, multi-day or monthly summaries.

Handling Regime Breaks and Non-Stationarity

Markets change. A state representation that works well in one regime may be misleading in another. While no preprocessing can fully solve this, some design choices help:

- Use rolling windows for normalization and factor estimation to adapt to changing volatility and correlation structures.
- Include regime indicators (such as volatility indices, credit spreads, or macro conditions) as part of the state so the agent can condition its policy on them.

- Periodically re-estimate neutralization regressions and orthogonalization transformations on recent data, not the full history.

The goal is to avoid "baking in" a particular historical regime into the state transformations themselves.

Example State Designs

We conclude with three example state designs that illustrate how these ideas play out in practice.

Long-Only Equity Fund

A long-only mutual fund investing in a broad equity universe might use:

- **Per-asset features:** cross-sectional ranks of value, momentum, quality, and size; 20-day volatility; 60-day beta to the index; all neutralized with respect to sectors and market beta.
- **Portfolio features:** current weights; sector and country exposures; active weight versus benchmark; recent active returns and tracking error estimates.
- **Horizon and frequency:** daily decisions with monthly lookback windows for some features; all signals lagged to avoid lookahead.

The RL agent learns to tilt the portfolio relative to a benchmark using neutralized alphas, while respecting sector and country constraints introduced later through the action and constraint mechanisms.

Long–Short Multi-Asset Book

A hedge-fund-style long–short book trading equities, futures, and FX might use:

- **Per-instrument features:** normalized carry, trend, value, and volatility carry signals; cross-asset correlation cluster indicators; liquidity proxies.
- **Neutralization:** cross-sectional regression to remove exposure to a small set of global risk factors (equity beta, term structure level, credit, dollar index).
- **Portfolio features:** gross and net exposure, leverage, concentration indices, and factor exposures from a multi-asset risk model.

Here neutralization helps the agent focus on *relative* value and diversified sources of return rather than re-leveraging the same global risk factors.

Macro Allocation Agent

A macro allocation agent trading country equity indices, bond futures, and FX may use:

- **Per-asset features:** macro-sensitive indicators such as growth surprises, inflation surprises, yield curve slopes, and valuation spreads; medium-horizon momentum.
- **Normalization:** z-scoring within country or asset class; ranking carry and value signals cross-sectionally.
- **Neutralization:** orthogonalization so that, for example, growth surprises are made orthogonal to inflation surprises and both are neutralized to global risk-on/off indicators.
- **Portfolio features:** country-level exposures, duration and FX risk, and measures of global risk appetite (such as equity volatility indices).

The resulting state allows the agent to make allocation decisions based on differentiated macro signals rather than simple "risk-on vs. risk-off" positions.

Signal integration and feature neutralization form the backbone of RL-based portfolio management. By carefully transforming raw market data and alpha factors into a stable, factor-aware state, we give the RL agent a fighting chance to learn genuinely useful allocation policies rather than artifacts of unclean data or hidden exposures. In the next sections, we will build on this state representation to specify how the agent acts on the portfolio, incorporates transaction costs, and respects risk and regulatory constraints.

4.2 End-to-End Allocation Agents

In the previous section we focused on the *state* of a portfolio RL problem: how to transform raw prices, factors, and alpha signals into a clean, factor-aware representation. We now turn to the other side of the Markov decision process: *what the agent does.* Given a state, how exactly does an RL agent act on a portfolio?

This section develops the notion of an *end-to-end allocation agent*: a policy that directly controls portfolio weights or trades, embedded in a realistic trading loop. We will:

- Define practical action spaces: target weights, weight changes, and trade quantities.
- Explain rebalancing policies: decision times, partial versus full rebalancing, and no-trade regions.
- Treat cash management explicitly: cash buffers, inflows/outflows, and over-allocation avoidance.
- Show how shorting permissions, borrow limits, and eligibility rules constrain the agent.
- Describe the transition dynamics that map actions to new portfolio states.
- Present design patterns for long-only funds, long–short books, and macro allocation agents.

The central idea is to clearly specify how the policy's outputs connect to real portfolio changes. This mapping must be expressive enough to capture interesting strategies, yet structured enough to make learning stable and economically plausible.

What Does an Allocation Action Look Like?

Once we have a state s_t that summarizes market conditions and current holdings, the policy must choose an *action* a_t. In portfolio management, it is helpful to think of a_t in three main parameterizations:

- **Target portfolio weights.**
- **Incremental changes in weights.**
- **Trade quantities in currency or units.**

Each choice leads to a different balance between simplicity, realism, and learning difficulty.

Action as Target Weights

In the target-weight formulation, the policy outputs a desired portfolio composition for the next period. For a universe of N assets (plus cash), the action is a vector:

$$a_t = \left(w_{1,t}^{target}, \ldots, w_{N,t}^{target}, w_{cash,t}^{target}\right),$$

subject to constraints such as weights summing to one and lying within bounds.

This is conceptually simple:

- The agent says, "I want 2% in stock 1, 1.5% in stock 2, ..., and 5% in cash."
- The trading engine computes trades needed to move from current weights to these targets.

Advantages:

- Easy to ensure feasibility (for example by passing raw outputs through a softmax and clipping).
- Naturally enforces a full investment constraint if desired.
- Fits long-only mutual funds and benchmark-relative strategies.

Disadvantages:

- Small changes in the target can imply large trades if the current portfolio is far away.
- The agent may overtrade if not explicitly penalized or regularized.

Action as Incremental Weight Changes

In the incremental formulation, the policy outputs how much to *move* each weight:

$$a_t = \big(\Delta w_{1,t}, \ldots, \Delta w_{N,t}\big).$$

These increments are then applied to the current weights, possibly with clipping and re-normalization.

Advantages:

- Naturally captures "small adjustment" behavior, especially under transaction costs.
- The magnitude of a_t directly reflects turnover pressure; it can be regularized or constrained.
- Smooths learning, since actions are relative to the existing portfolio.

Disadvantages:

- Requires an additional step to ensure that resulting weights are feasible and sum appropriately.
- May drift unintentionally if the agent systematically biases increments in one direction.

Action as Trade Quantities

The most realistic, but also most demanding, representation is to define actions as direct trades:

- Number of shares or contracts to buy or sell per instrument.
- Or, notional amounts (e.g., dollars of each asset).

Advantages:

- Matches real trading instructions ("buy 10,000 shares of stock A").
- Integrates neatly with transaction cost, execution, and impact models.
- Allows fine control over partial fills and order types in more advanced environments.

Disadvantages:

- State and reward must handle more complex mapping from orders to resulting holdings.
- Learning can be more difficult because the relationship between action scale and portfolio risk/return is less direct.

In practice, early prototypes often use target weights for simplicity, and later migrate to incremental or trade-based actions as the environment becomes more realistic.

From Policy Outputs to the MDP Loop

No matter which parameterization we choose, the policy is embedded in the same Markov decision process loop: observe state, act, environment transitions, and observe next state. It is useful to fix this picture explicitly, since it guides how we implement the environment and how we design the state and action interfaces.

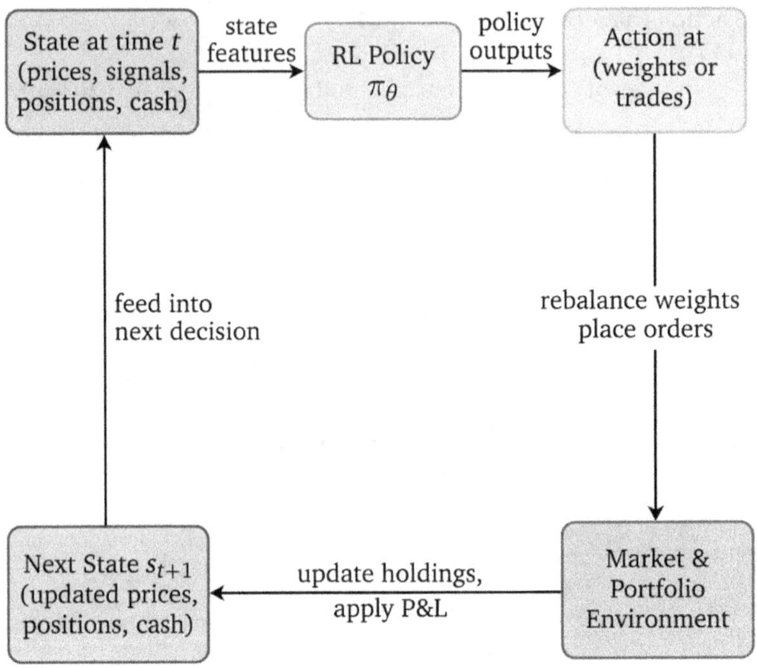

Right after explaining the action parameterizations, we can visualize this loop.

This schematic emphasizes that the *portfolio environment* is responsible for turning actions into trades, P&L, and updated positions, while the policy only manipulates a compact action representation.

Rebalancing Logic: When and How Much to Trade

An allocation agent does not act continuously; it acts at discrete decision times. Between these times the environment evolves passively:

prices move, P&L accumulates, and positions drift.

Decision Frequency

Typical choice of decision frequency includes:

- Daily close-to-close for medium-term factors.
- Hourly or every few minutes for intraday strategies.
- Single-step per episode for coarse asset allocation (e.g., monthly rebalancing).

Higher frequency gives more opportunities to react but also increases data requirements, transaction costs, and learning complexity. The decision frequency should match the horizon of the signals used in the state: slow signals do not justify ultra-high-frequency rebalancing.

Full versus Partial Rebalancing

- **Full rebalancing:** At each decision, the agent is allowed (and sometimes implicitly encouraged) to move directly from current holdings to its preferred targets. This is natural in the target-weight formulation.
- **Partial rebalancing:** The environment or policy can impose a cap on how much change is allowed per step, or the policy can output incremental moves. This reflects practical limitations such as market impact, risk constraints, or operational limits.

Partial rebalancing can be implemented by:

- Scaling large requested changes down to a maximum turnover per period.
- Interpreting policy outputs as desired *changes* rather than absolute targets.

No-Trade Regions and Minimum Trade Sizes

Real portfolio managers rarely rebalance for tiny changes, due to fixed costs and operational overhead. We can reflect this via:

- **No-trade thresholds:** If the difference between current and target weight is below a small epsilon, do nothing.
- **Minimum trade size:** Trades smaller than a given notional or share count are rounded down to zero.

These behaviors can be encoded:

- Directly in the environment: after receiving an action, apply rounding and thresholds.
- Indirectly via training: penalize small but non-zero trades in the reward function, encouraging the agent to either trade meaningfully or not at all.

In either case, modeling no-trade regions stabilizes learning by discouraging churning behavior that adds noise to the reward.

Cash Management and Over-Allocation Prevention

Many introductory RL portfolio formulations ignore cash, implicitly assuming that the agent is always exactly fully invested with no leftover capital or borrowing. In practice, cash plays at least three important roles:

- A buffer for trading frictions (spreads, fees, margin calls).
- A safe asset with low volatility.
- A bookkeeping mechanism to ensure actions do not allocate more than available capital.

Representing Cash in the Portfolio

We can treat cash as another asset in the universe:

- It has a (possibly small) return, such as a risk-free interest rate or overnight funding rate.
- It contributes to the total portfolio value and appears in state features.
- The agent can allocate more or less wealth to cash, subject to lower and upper bounds.

In a long-only mutual fund, cash might be constrained to stay between, say, 0% and 5% of the net asset value. In a hedge fund, cash balances can be negative (financing leveraged positions), subject to margin and funding constraints.

Maintaining Cash Buffers

The environment should ensure that capital is available to cover expected costs and margin requirements. Common rules include:

- Require a minimum cash buffer as a percentage of gross exposure.
- Automatically scale down requested positions if they would breach margin or cash limits.
- Penalize states where cash is too low or negative beyond allowed thresholds.

These rules protect the agent from repeatedly proposing infeasible reallocations, which would otherwise complicate training and distort the learning signal.

Handling Inflows and Outflows

For many real portfolios, capital is not fixed:

- Mutual funds experience subscriptions and redemptions.
- Institutional mandates may receive periodic contributions or withdrawals.

In an RL environment, inflows/outflows can be modeled as exogenous events:

- At certain steps, the environment changes the total portfolio value by adding or removing cash.
- The agent sees this through state variables such as cash balance and asset weights.
- Optional: inflow/outflow magnitudes can be part of the state so the agent anticipates them.

Including these events makes the environment more realistic and tests whether the policy is robust to changing capital.

Shorting, Leverage, and Eligibility Rules

Portfolio actions are also shaped by what kinds of positions are allowed:

- **Long-only:** Weights must be non-negative; shorting is prohibited.
- **Long–short:** Both long and short positions are permitted, possibly subject to total leverage and shorting limits.
- **Eligibility:** Some assets may be untradeable at certain times due to liquidity, mandates, or regulatory rules.

Encoding Long-Only Constraints

For long-only funds, we can:

- Parameterize actions via a non-negative transform (e.g., softmax) and interpret them as weights.
- Enforce a non-negative lower bound when applying incremental changes or trade-based actions.

This ensures that the environment never holds short positions due to numerical error or mis-specified actions.

Modeling Leverage and Shorting

For long–short books:

- The action or environment must track gross and net exposures.
- A leverage cap (e.g., gross exposure not exceeding 300% of net asset value) can be enforced by scaling down requested positions proportionally.
- Short positions require borrow availability; some assets may be non-shortable or more expensive to short, affecting costs and constraints.

The state should expose key leverage and exposure metrics so the agent understands the consequences of its decisions.

Asset Eligibility and Trading Halts

Real markets often have instruments that cannot be traded at a given time:

- Trading halts or suspensions.
- Liquidity constraints (e.g., penny stocks excluded from a mandate).
- Compliance restrictions (e.g., no sanctioned securities).

The environment can represent eligibility via a mask:

- At each decision time, some assets are marked as ineligible.
- Actions targeting ineligible assets are ignored or projected away.
- Eligibility indicators can be part of the state to avoid confusing the agent.

This mechanism also helps prototype execution constraints that will be revisited in the execution-focused chapters.

Transition Dynamics: From Action to Next State

Once an action is chosen, the environment must perform several steps before producing the next state:

- **Translate actions into orders or target weights.**
- **Apply trading rules:** no-trade thresholds, min size, eligibility masks, and leverage scaling.
- **Execute trades:** adjust holdings, cash, and possibly record transaction costs and impact.
- **Update prices:** advance the simulated market to the next time step.
- **Compute P&L and reward:** mark the portfolio to market and calculate the reward for the RL algorithm.
- **Construct the next state:** recompute features from updated prices, positions, and signals.

Even if transaction costs and impact are not yet modeled in detail (the focus of the next section), the environment should at minimum:

- Ensure that holdings and cash are internally consistent.
- Avoid impossible transitions (such as negative share counts in a long-only fund).

- Propagate changes in positions into the state so the agent receives feedback on its actions.

This consistent Markovian evolution is what allows RL algorithms to meaningfully associate actions with outcomes.

Design Patterns for Different Strategy Types

We close with three illustrative design patterns, each combining the aforementioned choices in a coherent way.

Long-Only Equity Fund

- **Action space:** Target weights for each stock plus cash, constrained to be non-negative and sum to one.
- **Rebalancing:** Daily decisions, with no-trade thresholds and capped turnover per day.
- **Cash:** Small mandatory buffer (e.g., 1–3%); automatic scaling of targets if proposed allocation exceeds available capital.
- **Constraints:** Sector and country bounds enforced via post-processing (projecting weights into a feasible set).

This setup closely matches how many benchmark-relative equity portfolios are run, and is relatively easy for RL algorithms to handle.

Long–Short Market-Neutral Book

- **Action space:** Incremental changes in asset weights, allowing both long and short positions.
- **Rebalancing:** Daily or intraday; changes clipped to respect turnover and leverage limits.
- **Cash and leverage:** Net exposure near zero; gross exposure capped (e.g., 200%); cash may become negative to finance shorts, but total borrowing limited.

- **Constraints:** Market neutrality enforced by scaling or projecting weights to zero beta; shorting eligibility masks applied to illiquid or restricted names.

The increment-based action space and explicit leverage constraints support more nuanced trading while keeping the environment manageable.

Macro Allocation Agent (Futures/ETFs)

- **Action space:** Trade quantities in contracts or notional for a small set of country indices, bond futures, and FX.
- **Rebalancing:** Weekly or monthly, matching the slower-moving macro signals in the state.
- **Cash and margin:** Futures positions require margin; the environment tracks required margin and liquidates or scales down if limits are breached.
- **Constraints:** Position limits per contract, overall risk limits in terms of duration, equity beta, and FX exposure.

Here, the emphasis is on matching the economic meaning of trades (e.g., "long duration in the US, short duration in Europe") with the action outputs, and handling the leverage inherent in derivatives.

End-to-end allocation agents close the loop between signals and trades. They take the factor-aware state engineered in earlier sections and translate it into concrete portfolio actions via a carefully designed action space, rebalancing policy, and cash and constraint management. By making these design choices explicit and grounded in real portfolio practice, we provide the structure that RL algorithms need to learn stable and economically meaningful allocation policies. The next sections will enrich this environment further by adding transaction costs, market impact, and explicit risk-aware objectives.

4.3 Transaction Costs, Impact, and Turnover Control

In the previous sections we assumed a frictionless world: whenever the allocation agent decided to change the portfolio, trades were executed instantaneously at observable prices, and the only source of randomness in rewards came from subsequent market moves. Real trading is very different. Every position change has a cost, and those costs can easily wipe out the edge of even strong alpha signals if they are ignored.

This section explains how to extend the RL portfolio environment to include realistic trading frictions and how to reflect them in the reward structure so that the agent learns to trade *just enough*, rather than as often as possible. We will:

- Decompose transaction costs into their main components.
- Introduce simple but useful models for slippage and market impact.
- Show how to embed these costs into the environment's transition dynamics and the RL reward.
- Define turnover and explain how to control it via penalties and action smoothing.
- Discuss inventory and concentration costs for illiquid or risky assets.
- Emphasize calibration and stress testing to avoid overfitting to optimistic assumptions.

Throughout, we keep the focus on intuition and implementation rather than on complex microstructure models. The goal is to capture the *first-order* economic effects that matter most for an allocation agent.

What Are Transaction Costs?

When you move from one portfolio to another, you do not simply exchange assets at mid prices. You typically cross the bid–ask spread, pay brokerage or exchange fees, and possibly move the market price against yourself if your order is large relative to available liquidity. These effects can be organized into:

- **Explicit costs:** easily observable or contractual costs:
  - Broker commissions.
  - Exchange and clearing fees.
  - Taxes or levies (e.g., stamp duty in some markets).
- **Implicit costs:** embedded in the prices at which you actually trade:
  - Bid–ask spread: you buy at the ask and sell at the bid.
  - Slippage: execution price worse than expected, even relative to bid/ask.
  - Market impact: your trade itself moves the price unfavorably.

In addition, certain positions create *inventory costs*:

- Financing costs for leveraged or short positions.
- Borrow fees for hard-to-borrow stocks.
- Risk capital charges or internal capital costs for large or concentrated positions.

An allocation-focused RL agent does not need a tick-by-tick execution simulator, but it must feel the economic weight of these costs whenever it trades. That is why we build approximate cost models directly into the environment's step function.

Modeling Transaction Costs in the Environment

Consider a decision at time t where the agent changes its holdings from h_t to h_{t+1} (expressed, for example, in shares or weights). Define the *trade vector* as:

$$\Delta h_t = h_{t+1} - h_t.$$

The cost associated with this trade is then a function of Δh_t, current prices, and liquidity conditions. The total transaction cost for the step is typically modeled as the sum of:

- A *spread* or *variable* component that grows roughly in proportion to the absolute traded volume.
- An *impact* component that grows faster than linearly with size relative to market volume.
- A *fixed* component (commissions, fees) that can be roughly proportional to the number of trades or their notional size.

We can think of the per-asset cost as:

$$\text{cost}_i(\Delta h_{i,t}) \approx \text{spread term} + \text{impact term} + \text{fees}.$$

Spread and Slippage

A simple model for spread-related costs is to assume that whenever you buy, you pay half the spread above the mid price; whenever you sell, you receive half the spread below the mid. If $S_{i,t}$ is the bid–ask spread for asset i at time t and $p_{i,t}$ is the mid price, then the cost due to spread for trading $\Delta h_{i,t}$ shares is approximately:

$$\text{spread cost}_{i,t} \approx \frac{S_{i,t}}{2} \cdot |\Delta h_{i,t}|.$$

Slippage can be incorporated by multiplying this term by a factor greater than one, or by adding a small additional term proportional to trade size. For daily or lower-frequency RL simulations, it is often sufficient to use a constant fractional spread per asset or per asset class calibrated from historical execution data.

Market Impact

Market impact captures the idea that large orders move prices against you. A widely used stylized model assumes that the impact cost increases with the *square root* of the ratio of your trade size to typical daily volume:

$$\text{impact cost}_{i,t} \propto p_{i,t} \cdot |\Delta h_{i,t}| \cdot \sqrt{\frac{|\Delta h_{i,t}|}{\text{ADV}_{i,t}}},$$

where $\text{ADV}_{i,t}$ is the average daily volume (in shares or notional) for asset i.

The exact functional form is less important than the qualitative behavior:

- Small trades relative to volume incur almost linear costs (dominated by spreads and small impact).
- Very large trades become disproportionately expensive.

This nonlinearity is crucial for RL: it discourages the agent from making massive one-shot reallocations and encourages more gradual trading when necessary.

Inventory and Financing Costs

Inventory-related costs can be modeled as ongoing charges that depend on the size and composition of the holdings, even if no trade takes place at a given step. For example:

- **Short borrow fees:** for a short position in stock i of size $h_{i,t} < 0$, charge a daily fee proportional to $|h_{i,t}|$ and the borrow rate for that stock.
- **Financing cost for leverage:** if the gross exposure or margin usage exceeds a threshold, apply an extra cost on the leveraged portion, reflecting higher funding costs.
- **Concentration penalties:** if an asset or sector weight exceeds a certain level, apply a risk capital charge per unit of time.

These costs turn holding extreme positions into an explicit trade-off that the agent experiences continually, not only when it rebalances.

Embedding Costs into the RL Reward

The environment's reward should reflect *net* performance from the investor's point of view. At a basic level, we can decompose the reward r_t as:

$$r_t = \text{gross portfolio return}_t - \text{transaction costs}_t - \text{inventory costs}_t.$$

In a step-by-step simulation:

1. The agent proposes an action a_t, which is translated into desired trades.
2. The environment computes Δh_t, executes trades at execution prices, and deducts explicit and implicit costs from cash.
3. The portfolio is marked to market at time $t+1$, yielding the gross return.
4. Inventory and financing charges for the period $[t, t+1]$ are computed from holdings.
5. The reward is the change in portfolio value during the period, net of all these costs.

This approach lets the RL algorithm directly experience the trade-off between return and cost: if it churns the portfolio for tiny expected alpha, the cost term dominates and the reward deteriorates.

Immediate Penalties vs. Horizon-Level Objectives

While net return per step is the most natural reward, we sometimes wish to adjust or augment it. Two common perspectives are:

- **Immediate penalties:** simply subtract costs at each step, as described above. This is intuitive and ensures that the temporal credit assignment for costs is clear: each action is immediately punished according to its cost.

- **Horizon-level optimization:** in some formulations, the objective may emphasize long-horizon net performance statistics (such as terminal wealth or multi-period Sharpe ratio). In practice, such objectives are still implemented using per-step rewards that include cost penalties, but the RL algorithm evaluates long-horizon returns when updating the policy.

For most allocation problems, combining per-step net returns with an episodic performance metric (for evaluation and possibly reward shaping) provides a good balance between interpretability and learning efficiency.

Turnover as a Controllable Quantity

Transaction costs are tightly linked to *turnover*: how much of the portfolio is traded per period. If we define the portfolio weights before and after rebalancing as w_t and w_{t+1}, a simple turnover measure for period t is:

$$\text{turnover}_t = \frac{1}{2} \sum_i |w_{i,t+1} - w_{i,t}|.$$

The factor $\frac{1}{2}$ ensures that turning over the entire portfolio from one set of assets to completely different ones gives a turnover of 100%.

Even when costs are explicitly modeled in the reward, it is often helpful to also penalize turnover directly, for three reasons:

- Turnover is a simple, stable proxy for cost, especially when cost estimates are noisy or uncertain.
- Many investment mandates and risk policies explicitly cap turnover.
- Penalizing turnover smooths actions, which can improve RL stability.

Turnover Penalties in the Reward

A common pattern is to modify the per-step reward as:

$$r_t^{\text{penalized}} = r_t^{\text{net}} - \lambda_{to} \cdot \text{turnover}_t,$$

where r_t^{net} already includes explicit cost deductions, and λ_{to} is a hyperparameter controlling the strength of the turnover penalty.

Intuitively:

- With $\lambda_{to} = 0$, the agent only cares about modeled costs. If these are underestimated, the learned policy may still trade too much.
- With larger λ_{to}, the agent is encouraged to trade only when it expects a sufficiently large improvement in future returns.

Action Smoothing and No-Trade Zones

Turnover control can also be implemented at the action level:

- **Action smoothing:** interpolate between the requested action and the current portfolio:

  $$w_{t+1} = (1 - \alpha)w_t + \alpha\, w_t^{\text{target}},$$

  where $\alpha \in (0, 1]$ controls how aggressively the agent can move towards its target. Smaller α means slower rebalancing and lower turnover.
- **No-trade zones:** if the requested change in a weight is below a threshold, ignore it and leave the position unchanged. This introduces a region around the current portfolio where the agent does not trade.

These mechanisms make trading frictions more transparent to the agent: small, noisy changes in its outputs will not always result in trades, and therefore will not always produce cost penalties.

Interplay Between Signal Noise, Frequency, and Costs

The value of trading depends on the *quality* of the information in the state and on how often signals change. Three basic principles are useful when designing RL portfolio environments:

- **Noisy signals + high costs + high frequency** is a recipe for overtrading and poor performance. The agent will see many apparent opportunities that are actually noise, pay costs frequently, and find it hard to improve on a passive benchmark.
- **Stable signals + moderate costs + moderate frequency** is often a good starting point for RL: the environment rewards patient exploitation of genuine edges.
- **Very low costs** (e.g., assuming free trading) will lead the agent to behave unrealistically, even if it fits the historical data well. Such policies are fragile when deployed with real-world costs.

From a design perspective, it is often beneficial to:

- Start with conservative (higher) cost assumptions than historical averages.
- Tune decision frequency to match the horizon of the strongest signals in the state.
- Use turnover penalties to further discourage marginal trades.

This encourages the algorithm to discover robust, low-churn policies that stand a better chance of surviving model errors and changing market conditions.

Inventory and Concentration Control

In addition to per-trade costs, many institutions care about inventory and concentration risk. These are particularly salient for:

- Portfolios trading illiquid stocks or credit instruments.
- Derivative strategies with large notional exposures.
- Books with strict regulatory or internal risk capital limits.

We can reflect these concerns in the environment and reward:

Illiquid Names and Position Limits

For illiquid assets, trading costs are higher and position sizes must be limited:

- Set higher spread and impact parameters for illiquid assets, based on their average volume and historical slippage.
- Impose maximum position sizes as a fraction of average daily volume or market capitalization.
- Penalize or prohibit trades that would exceed these position limits.

This naturally drives the RL agent to allocate more capital to liquid assets where its trades have smaller price effects.

Concentration and Risk Capital Charges

Concentration can be handled by:

- Adding a per-step penalty that increases with the maximum single-name weight or with concentration indices (for example, Herfindahl–Hirschman Index of weights).
- Making this penalty stronger for less liquid or riskier assets.

These penalties operate similarly to transaction costs, but apply continuously while the position is held, rather than only when trades occur. They push the agent towards more diversified portfolios, which is often both prudent and required by mandates.

Calibration and Stress Testing

All cost and impact models we have described are approximations. Their parameters—spreads, impact coefficients, fee schedules, borrow rates, and so on—must be calibrated from data or expert judgment.

Calibrating Cost Parameters

Practical approaches to calibration include:

- Using historical trade and quote data (if available) to estimate realized spreads, slippage, and impact as a function of order size and market conditions.
- For backtests without proprietary execution data, using conservative rules of thumb (e.g., a few basis points per side for liquid large-cap equities, higher for small caps or emerging markets).
- Differentiating cost parameters across asset classes: equities, futures, FX, and credit have very different liquidity and fee structures.

It is better to err on the side of overestimating costs: a policy that is profitable under pessimistic cost assumptions is more likely to survive in live trading.

Stress Testing Policies Under Different Cost Scenarios

Once an RL policy has been trained, it should be evaluated under several cost scenarios:

- **Base case:** the same cost model used for training.
- **High-cost scenario:** spreads, slippage, and impact parameters scaled up.
- **Low-liquidity scenario:** volumes reduced, making the same trades more impactful.

We can examine how:

- Cumulative net returns degrade as costs rise.
- Turnover and trading patterns change.
- The policy remains profitable or fails under stress.

If performance collapses with only modest cost increases, this indicates that the learned strategy relies heavily on fine-tuned assumptions and may be too fragile for deployment.

Transaction costs, market impact, and inventory penalties are not minor corrections; they are central to the real economics of trading. For an RL allocation agent, they shape the environment and the reward in ways that fundamentally change what "good" behavior looks like. By explicitly modeling spreads, slippage, impact, and inventory costs, and by controlling turnover through penalties and action smoothing, we encourage the agent to seek strategies that are not just profitable in theory, but also implementable and robust in practice. In the next section, we will integrate these cost-aware dynamics with risk-aware objectives and explicit portfolio constraints, completing the picture of a realistic RL-driven portfolio management system.

4.4 Risk-Aware Objectives and Constraint Handling

So far, our RL portfolio agent has been mainly rewarded for *return*: first ignoring frictions, then accounting for transaction costs and impact. In practice, any professionally managed portfolio is judged at least as much by its *risk* and its adherence to limits as by its raw performance. A strategy that occasionally doubles capital but frequently suffers 50% drawdowns or breaches leverage limits is usually unacceptable, no matter how impressive the backtest.

This section explains how to move from pure return maximization to *risk-aware* and *constraint-respecting* RL. We will:

- Introduce common risk-sensitive objectives: mean–variance, Sharpe, drawdown, VaR, and CVaR.
- Discuss how to approximate these objectives from simulated trajectories.
- Show how to encode practical constraints (leverage, exposures, position bounds, margin) into the RL framework.

- Present constrained Markov decision processes (CMDPs) and Lagrangian methods for handling multiple constraints.
- Describe safe-RL techniques such as shielding and early aborts in simulation.
- Provide design recipes that combine risk-aware rewards with explicit constraints for different portfolio types.

The overarching theme is that risk and constraints are not an afterthought; they must be built into both the objective and the environment from the start.

From Return-Only to Risk-Aware Objectives

In classical portfolio theory, risk and return are two sides of the same coin. RL is no different: if we only reward high average returns, the agent is incentivized to take as much risk as possible, including tail risk, as long as it helps the average. To moderate this behavior, we introduce risk-sensitive criteria.

Mean–Variance and Sharpe Ratio

The mean–variance framework measures performance by expected return and variance of return. The Sharpe ratio refines this by scaling excess return (over a risk-free rate) by volatility:

$$\text{Sharpe} \approx \frac{\mathbb{E}[R]}{\sqrt{\mathbb{V}[R]}}.$$

In an episodic RL setting (for example, simulating several years of trading per episode), we can estimate these quantities from the sequence of net returns within each episode. Two practical ways to use them are:

- **Episode-level objective:** treat the Sharpe ratio (or a simple mean–variance score like $\mathbb{E}[R] - \lambda\mathbb{V}[R]$) of the entire episode as a scalar return and use policy-gradient methods that work with episodic objectives.

- **Step-level shaping:** penalize realized variance at each step, for instance
$$r_t^{risk} = r_t^{net} - \lambda_{risk} \cdot \widehat{\sigma}_t^2,$$
where $\widehat{\sigma}_t$ is an estimate of current or predicted portfolio volatility.

Episode-level objectives capture the global trade-off between return and volatility more faithfully, but can make learning noisier and slower. Step-level shaping is easier to implement with standard off-the-shelf RL algorithms.

Drawdown-Sensitive Objectives

Investors care deeply about *drawdowns*—the peak-to-trough declines in portfolio value. Sharpe ratio treats upside and downside fluctuations symmetrically, whereas many investors are much more sensitive to downside.

In simulation, we can track:

- The running maximum portfolio value.
- The current drawdown as the percentage drop from this peak.
- The maximum drawdown over the episode.

There are two ways to encourage small drawdowns:

- **Penalize large drawdowns in the reward:** for example, subtract a penalty whenever the current drawdown exceeds some comfort threshold, or subtract a term at the end of the episode proportional to the maximum drawdown.
- **Risk-constrained formulation:** treat maximum drawdown as a constraint that must stay below a specified limit with high probability, and use constrained RL machinery to enforce it (discussed later).

Drawdown-sensitive shaping helps align the agent's behavior with investors who are more willing to miss some upside than to endure deep losses.

Downside Risk: VaR and CVaR

Value-at-Risk (VaR) and Conditional Value-at-Risk (CVaR) focus on the *left tail* of the return distribution:

- VaR at level α is a threshold such that returns are worse than this only with probability α (e.g., the 5% worst loss).
- CVaR at level α is the expected loss given that you are in that worst α fraction of outcomes.

In RL, we rarely estimate VaR or CVaR from a single episode, since that would be very noisy. Instead, we:

- Collect returns from many trajectories generated under the current policy.
- Empirically estimate VaR and CVaR by sorting or using robust tail estimators.
- Use these estimates to:
  - Construct a risk-aware objective (e.g., maximize mean return minus a multiple of CVaR).
  - Define constraints (e.g., CVaR must not exceed a given threshold) and apply constrained RL.

CVaR is particularly amenable to optimization because it is a coherent risk measure and can be handled with auxiliary variables and gradient-based procedures.

Encoding Practical Portfolio Constraints

Real portfolios face many constraints beyond the choice of risk measure. These constraints can be broadly categorized as:

- **Position constraints:** bounds on individual asset weights (e.g., 0%–3% per stock), long-only or long–short rules, minimum lot sizes.

- **Exposure constraints:** limits on sector, country, factor, or style exposures; net and gross exposure caps.
- **Leverage and margin constraints:** caps on gross exposure relative to capital, margin requirements for leveraged and derivative positions.
- **Risk constraints:** maximum volatility, drawdown, VaR, or CVaR over certain horizons.

We now discuss how to represent and enforce these constraints in an RL portfolio environment.

Hard vs. Soft Constraints

We distinguish:

- **Hard constraints:** must never be violated in simulation. For example, a mutual fund may be legally prohibited from shorting, or from exceeding a leverage of 100%.
- **Soft constraints:** violations are allowed in principle but are heavily discouraged or costly, such as mild sector overweights or temporary breaches of volatility targets.

In RL terms:

- Hard constraints are enforced by *projecting* actions or states into a feasible region.
- Soft constraints are typically handled by *penalty terms* in the reward or via CMDP formulations with associated cost signals.

Action Projection for Hard Constraints

Suppose the policy outputs a vector of target weights that may violate simple constraints such as non-negativity, maximum per-asset weight, or a leverage cap. The environment can apply an *action projection* step:

1. Start with the raw action (e.g., proposed weights).
2. Solve a small optimization problem that is as close as possible to the raw action (in some distance sense) but satisfies all hard constraints.
3. Use this projected action to update the portfolio.

For example:

- In a long-only fund, negative weights are set to zero and remaining weights are renormalized to sum to one.
- If a leverage cap is exceeded, all positions are scaled down proportionally until the cap is met.

This guarantees feasibility in every simulated step. The policy gradually learns that directions which are always projected away are useless, and it adapts by keeping its outputs closer to the feasible set.

Penalty Shaping for Soft Constraints

For soft constraints, we add penalty terms to the reward. Suppose we want to limit sector exposure to a range around a benchmark. Let c_t measure the degree of violation at time t (for example, how far a sector exposure exceeds its allowed band). The penalized reward becomes:

$$r_t^{penalized} = r_t^{net} - \lambda_c \cdot c_t,$$

where λ_c controls the trade-off between return and constraint adherence.

Similar penalties can be defined for:

- Volatility above a target level.
- Drawdown beyond a comfort threshold.
- Deviations from net exposure or beta neutrality.

Choosing the penalty strengths is partly an art: too small and the agent may ignore the constraint; too large and learning may collapse if the agent receives mostly negative rewards early on. A practical approach is to start with moderate penalties, monitor constraint violations in simulation, and iterate.

Constrained MDPs and Lagrangian Methods

When constraints are central to the problem—for example, keeping CVaR below a regulatory limit or leverage within strict bounds—it is useful to adopt a more formal framework: the *constrained Markov decision process* (CMDP).

CMDP Formulation

In a CMDP, the agent seeks to maximize expected cumulative reward subject to constraints on expected cumulative *costs*. Concretely:

- The environment produces a main reward r_t and one or more cost signals $c_t^{(k)}$, each associated with a constraint, such as:
  - $c_t^{(1)}$ = leverage over a threshold.
  - $c_t^{(2)}$ = sector exposure violation.
  - $c_t^{(3)}$ = tail-loss indicator beyond a VaR level.
- The objective is to:
  - Maximize $\mathbb{E}\left[\sum_t r_t\right]$,
  - Subject to $\mathbb{E}\left[\sum_t c_t^{(k)}\right] \leq d_k$ for each constraint k, where d_k are allowed budgets.

This formulation explicitly separates the role of performance and constraints, rather than mixing everything into a single scalar reward.

Lagrangian Relaxation

A standard way to solve CMDPs is to convert them into an unconstrained problem using *Lagrange multipliers.* We introduce non-negative multipliers λ_k and define the Lagrangian reward:

$$\tilde{r}_t = r_t - \sum_k \lambda_k c_t^{(k)}.$$

For fixed multipliers, maximizing expected cumulative $\tilde{r}_t$ is just a standard RL problem. The key is then to adjust the multipliers λ_k so that the resulting policy satisfies the constraints (on average). The process alternates between:

1. Policy improvement using RL on the current Lagrangian reward.

2. Multiplier updates: if a constraint is violated (average cost above d_k), increase λ_k; if it is comfortably satisfied, decrease λ_k.

Over time, this dual update balances the desire for higher returns against the need to respect constraints.

Geometric Intuition

It is helpful to visualize this process geometrically: the unconstrained RL problem seeks the global maximum of a performance landscape without any restrictions. The constrained problem restricts attention to a *feasible region* defined by constraints. The Lagrangian method effectively tilts the objective landscape using multipliers so that the optimum within the feasible region becomes the optimum of the modified objective.

Diagrammatic representation:

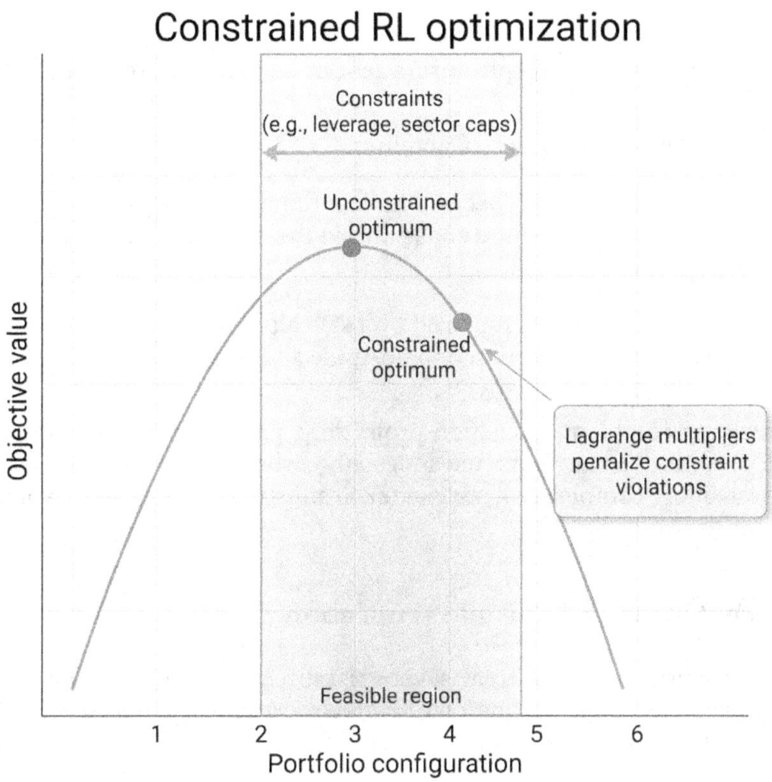

This figure is not to scale, but it reinforces the idea that constrained RL is about optimizing within a region defined by risk limits, not just driving the objective as high as possible anywhere.

Safe-RL Techniques for Portfolio Risk

Beyond shaping rewards and using CMDPs, several practical techniques can improve safety and constraint satisfaction in RL-based portfolio management.

Action Shielding

Action shielding intercepts unsafe actions before they are applied:

- The policy proposes an action.
- A *shield* module checks whether the action would violate any hard risk or exposure constraint in the next state (using approximate calculations).
- If so, the action is replaced by a safe alternative, such as the closest feasible projection or a no-trade action.

Shielding complements action projection: projection focuses on simple structural constraints (like long-only), whereas shielding can incorporate more complex risk metrics (such as estimated post-trade volatility or drawdown risk).

Early Aborts and Episode Truncation

In simulation, we can treat severe risk breaches (e.g., leverage well above allowed maximums or drawdown exceeding an unacceptably large limit) as *terminal events*:

- When a breach occurs, the episode ends immediately.
- The agent receives a large negative terminal reward.

Over time, the agent learns to avoid states that put it at risk of early termination. This approach mirrors real-world situations where severe breaches can lead to forced liquidation or mandate termination.

Conservative Value Function Estimation

Value-based RL methods estimate expected future returns from a given state. When constraints are present, especially tail-risk constraints, it is often better to err on the side of caution:

- Use lower confidence bounds on value estimates when choosing actions (e.g., pessimistic estimates that assume adverse future shocks).
- Incorporate risk-aware value estimates that focus on downside outcomes (e.g., minimizing worst-case or CVaR of returns).

These techniques reduce the temptation for the agent to exploit optimistic estimation errors in the value function to justify risky behavior.

Design Recipes for Risk-Aware Portfolio Agents

We summarize with two concrete design patterns that blend risk-aware rewards and constraint handling.

Long-Only Mutual Fund with Tight Drawdown Budget

- **Objective:** maximize long-horizon net return with an approximate Sharpe penalty and an explicit drawdown penalty at the episode level.
- **Hard constraints:** long-only, maximum position size (e.g., 3% per stock), sector and country bounds, leverage capped at 100%.
- **Soft constraints:** tracking error to benchmark within a target range, modest volatility target.
- **Implementation:**
  - Project actions into a long-only, benchmark-relative feasible set.
  - Add per-step penalties when volatility or tracking error exceed desired ranges.
  - Penalize large drawdowns at the end of each episode.
  - Use episode-level evaluation metrics focused on downside risk, such as maximum drawdown and CVaR of active returns.

This design encourages smooth, benchmark-aware allocations that respect investor tolerance for losses.

Leveraged Long–Short Book with Exposure and CVaR Limits

- **Objective:** maximize expected net return subject to constraints on:
  - Gross leverage (e.g., $\leq 300\%$),
  - Net exposure (e.g., between -20% and $+20\%$),
  - Sector exposure ranges,
  - 5% CVaR of periodic returns below a specified threshold.
- **CMDP formulation:** treat leverage, net exposure, sector exposures, and CVaR exceedance as separate cost signals with budgets.
- **Implementation:**
  - Use Lagrangian RL: maintain multipliers for each constraint and update them based on observed violations.
  - Project actions to satisfy simple structural constraints (e.g., no individual position above a given notional).
  - Apply shielding to reject actions that would cause immediate leverage or margin breaches.
  - Evaluate policies under multiple stress scenarios for volatility and liquidity.

This setup aligns well with hedge-fund mandates where sophisticated risk targets and limits are as central as performance.

Risk-aware objectives and constraint handling transform RL from an academic exercise into a framework that can support real institutional portfolios. By enriching the reward with volatility, drawdown, and tail-risk considerations, and by encoding leverage, exposure, and position limits as hard or soft constraints within a CMDP, we guide the learning process towards strategies that respect investor risk appetite and regulatory requirements. In combination with the cost-aware dynamics developed earlier, these techniques bring us close to a realistic RL-driven portfolio management system that seeks not only high returns but also resilience and discipline.

Chapter 5

Smart Trade Execution with Reinforcement Learning

Execution is where beautiful backtests go to die-or to outperform. In this chapter, we turn trading signals into concrete order schedules and placements, using reinforcement learning to navigate limit order books, dark pools, and milliseconds of latency so that your intended P&L actually reaches the bottom line.

5.1 Execution Benchmarks and Optimal Scheduling

In earlier chapters we focused on deciding *what* portfolio to hold and *when* to change it. In practice, there is a second, equally important problem: *how* to trade from the current position to the desired one in real markets without giving away unnecessary edge.

This section introduces the language practitioners use to judge execution quality and then builds up the classical optimal execution framework. That framework will later serve as the natural baseline and "teacher" for reinforcement learning (RL) agents, which you can think of as data-driven schedulers that adapt execution in real time instead of following a fixed pre-computed plan.

We proceed in three steps:

- Define standard execution benchmarks and objectives.
- Explain the trade-off between market impact and schedule risk.
- Show how optimal execution can be viewed as a sequential decision problem, paving the way to RL.

Execution Quality and Benchmarks

Suppose a portfolio manager decides at 10:00 a.m. to buy 500,000 shares of a stock by 3:30 p.m. That block order is called the *parent order*. The desk will execute it through many *child orders* throughout the day.

Even if the trading algorithm is completely honest and tries its best, the realized average price will almost never match the "ideal" price the manager had in mind when approving the trade. The difference between those two is called *implementation shortfall.* To measure and improve execution, desks agree on explicit benchmarks.

TWAP: Time-Weighted Average Price

Time-Weighted Average Price (TWAP) is the simplest target. The trading horizon is divided into N equal time buckets (e.g., every 5 minutes). The benchmark price is the simple average of prices across those buckets:

$$\text{TWAP} = \frac{1}{N}\sum_{k=1}^{N} P_{t_k}.$$

A TWAP execution strategy typically trades the same quantity in each time bucket:

$$q_k^{TWAP} = \frac{Q}{N}, \quad k = 1, \ldots, N,$$

where Q is the total order size.

TWAP is:

- *Simple and transparent*: easy to explain to clients and regulators.
- *Liquidity-ignoring*: it does not care whether the market is currently thick or thin.
- *Often a baseline*: many more sophisticated algorithms are compared against TWAP in transaction cost analysis (TCA).

VWAP: Volume-Weighted Average Price

In most markets, trading activity is not uniform over the day. There is usually a U-shaped pattern: heavy volume near the open and close, thinner volume mid-day. Volume-Weighted Average Price (VWAP) adjusts to this reality.

If V_{t_k} is the total market volume in bucket k, then:

$$\mathrm{VWAP} = \frac{\sum_{k=1}^{N} P_{t_k} V_{t_k}}{\sum_{k=1}^{N} V_{t_k}}.$$

A VWAP execution strategy trades in proportion to market volume:

$$q_k^{VWAP} = Q \cdot \frac{V_{t_k}}{\sum_{\ell=1}^{N} V_{t_\ell}}.$$

VWAP is:

- *Liquidity-aware*: it sends more volume when the market is more liquid.
- *Market standard*: many institutional mandates and broker algorithms are expressed relative to VWAP.
- *Still blind to price dynamics*: VWAP does not explicitly model price impact, volatility, or directional drift.

Arrival Price and Implementation Shortfall

Managers care about the price at which they *decide* to trade. This is called the *arrival price*, denoted P_0. One common definition is the mid-quote at the time the order is released.

If the realized average execution price for a buy order is P_{exec}, then the *implementation shortfall* in currency units is:

$$\text{IS} = Q \cdot (P_{\text{exec}} - P_0).$$

For a sell order, the sign is reversed; in all cases, *positive* shortfall means worse performance than the arrival price.

Implementation shortfall decomposes conceptually into:

- **Spread cost**: crossing the bid-ask spread when using market orders.
- **Market impact**: the price move caused by the order itself.
- **Market drift**: the "background" move that would have happened even if you had not traded.
- **Residual error and noise**: slippage due to timing, latency, and randomness in fills.

In this section, we keep the focus on impact and risk; latency and infrastructure will be handled later in the chapter.

From Benchmarks to Optimal Schedules

TWAP and VWAP give simple schedules but ignore a key tension. Trading *too fast* causes large market impact. Trading *too slow* exposes you to price risk: the market may drift against you while you wait. Optimal execution models formalize this trade-off.

We consider a single-asset buy order of size Q to be completed over a horizon $[0, T]$, split into N intervals of length $\Delta t = T/N$. Let x_k be the remaining inventory *after* trading in interval k; thus $x_0 = Q$ and $x_N = 0$. The trade in interval k is:

$$v_k = x_{k-1} - x_k,$$

interpreted as shares traded (positive for buys).

Price Dynamics with Impact

A simple yet powerful model writes the *unaffected* price (what the price would be without our trading) as:

$$P_k^{\text{unaff}} = P_{k-1}^{\text{unaff}} + \sigma\sqrt{\Delta t}\,\varepsilon_k,$$

where ε_k are independent shocks with mean zero and variance one, and σ represents volatility.

Our trading affects prices in two ways:

- **Temporary impact**: we pay a worse price when we trade aggressively, but the effect mostly fades by the next period.
- **Permanent impact**: part of the move induced by our trade persists and shifts the future mid-price.

A widely used linear impact model writes the execution price in interval k as

$$P_k^{\text{exec}} = P_{k-1} + \eta v_k + \gamma x_{k-1},$$

where

- η controls the temporary (per-share) impact of the trade v_k,
- γ controls the permanent impact proportional to remaining inventory.

This structure captures two intuitive ideas:

- Larger, more aggressive trades move the price more within the period (temporary impact).
- Large remaining inventory exerts a persistent pressure on the price (permanent impact).

Cost and Risk of a Schedule

The total (implementation) cost of following a schedule $\{x_k\}_{k=0}^{N}$ is the sum over all intervals of shares traded times the execution price:

$$\text{Cost} = \sum_{k=1}^{N} v_k P_k^{\text{exec}}.$$

Using the linear impact model and taking expectations with respect to the price shocks, we can separate the *expected* cost from its *variance*:

- The expected cost captures systematic effects like impact.
- The variance captures exposure to price risk due to volatility during the schedule.

With linear impact, the expected cost becomes a quadratic function of the trade sizes $\{v_k\}$ (or equivalently, of the inventory path $\{x_k\}$). Meanwhile, the cost variance is proportional to the sum of squared inventories, because holding more shares for longer keeps you exposed to volatility. Intuitively:

$$\text{Risk} \propto \sigma^2 \sum_{k=1}^{N} x_k^2 \Delta t.$$

So a schedule that front-loads trading (finishes early) has *less* risk but potentially more impact (due to larger early trades), while a schedule that spreads out trading more evenly has *less* impact but more risk.

The Schedule-Risk vs. Market-Impact Trade-off

The classical Almgren-Chriss framework combines these two components into a single objective. For a risk-averse trader, a natural criterion is:

$$\min_{\{x_k\}} \quad \mathbb{E}[\text{Cost}] + \lambda \cdot \text{Var}[\text{Cost}],$$

subject to $x_0 = Q$, $x_N = 0$, and x_k non-increasing.

Here λ is a risk-aversion coefficient:

- If λ is very small, you care mostly about minimizing expected cost (impact).
- If λ is large, you are willing to pay more impact to reduce risk.

Under linear assumptions, this optimization problem has a closed-form solution: the optimal inventory trajectory $\{x_k^*\}$ forms a smooth curve from Q down to 0. The shape of that curve depends on the parameters:

- Higher volatility σ pushes you to *trade faster* to reduce risk.
- Stronger impact (larger η or γ) pushes you to *trade more gently*, spreading out the order.
- Higher risk-aversion λ makes the schedule more front-loaded; lower λ makes it flatter.

It is useful to contrast the optimal schedule to TWAP and VWAP under the same conditions. In a calm, highly liquid market with low impact and low volatility, all three schedules may look similar. In a volatile, low-liquidity environment, the optimal schedule can differ sharply, often trading much more aggressively early on than TWAP or VWAP would, especially for a risk-averse trader.

```
import python as pt
from python.insport import ptv

def execution schedules(Q, -Q):
    order = order.time.recuver(t, Q)
    VWAP-like = order'Optimal (high risk aversion)
    TWAP  = Optimal.jorder Optimal, (low risk aversion)
    inventory = optimal(inventory '- - '')
    chart = VWAP-like((optimal, Q) + 1)

chart = horder.execution schedules.chart(Q)
print('Time within 0)
```

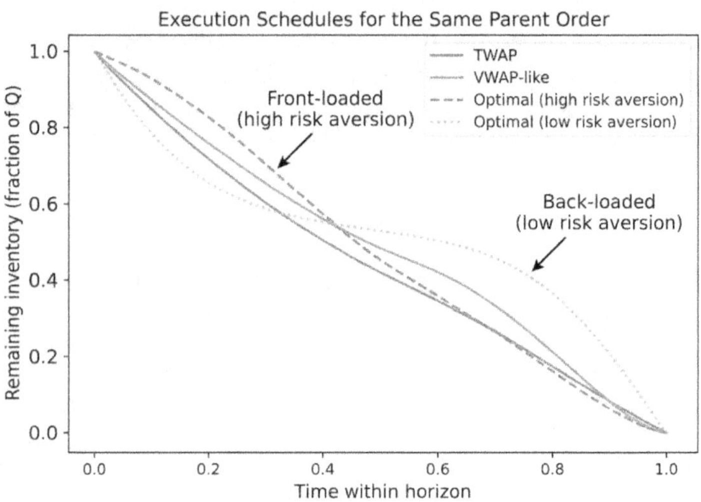

This figure emphasizes that:

- TWAP ignores both liquidity and risk; it is simply a straight line.
- VWAP adapts to typical volume patterns but not to volatility or risk preferences.
- Optimal schedules tilt earlier or later depending on risk aversion and market conditions.

Practical Constraints on Schedules

Real-world execution cannot follow arbitrary mathematical curves. Schedules are constrained by market rules and risk controls. Important examples include:

Participation caps. Many buy-side firms limit how much of the market's trading volume they are willing to represent at any point in time, e.g., "do not exceed 20% of total volume." This cap prevents the algorithm from becoming the market. Mathematically, if V_k is expected market volume in interval k and ρ_{max} is the cap, then we must have

$$v_k \leq \rho_{max} V_k.$$

No-trade intervals and blackout periods. Certain times of day (e.g., auction periods, news releases, or regulatory blackout windows) may be excluded or constrained. This introduces hard constraints on which k can have positive v_k.

Tick size and lot constraints. Shares must be integral, and prices must lie on tick grids. For a very small-cap stock, you cannot trade tiny fractions of the order in each interval; the schedule must respect minimum size increments.

Exchange-specific rules. Different venues have different auction mechanisms, market-making obligations, or dark-pool rules. Some schedules might be legal and executed smoothly on one venue but problematic on another.

All of these constraints turn the clean algebra of the optimal schedule into a constrained optimization problem. The theoretical curve from the Almgren-Chriss model becomes a *target* that must be adapted in real time.

From Optimal Execution to Sequential Decisions

So far we have treated the execution problem as if we could decide the entire schedule at time 0, based on model parameters and expectations. In practice, the environment changes throughout the day:

- Spreads widen or narrow.

- Order book depth fluctuates.
- News breaks and volatility spikes.
- Hidden liquidity appears in dark pools.

A pre-computed schedule cannot react to these changes unless we periodically re-solve the optimization problem with updated inputs. Conceptually, this is exactly a sequential decision problem:

- At each decision time t_k, you observe the current market state: prices, spreads, depths, recent trades, remaining time, remaining inventory, and so on.
- You choose an action: how much to trade, with which order type, and on which venue.
- The market responds: your orders are filled (or not), the price moves, liquidity changes.
- You receive a contribution to your execution cost and update your remaining inventory.

Formally, this is the structure of a Markov Decision Process (MDP):

- **State** s_k: includes remaining inventory, time-to-deadline, and market variables.
- **Action** a_k: determines trade size and (later) order type and venue.
- **Transition**: from (s_k, a_k) to s_{k+1} driven by the stochastic evolution of prices and order book.
- **Reward**: typically the negative of execution cost (or incremental shortfall) in that interval.

The classical optimal execution model corresponds to solving this MDP *analytically* under strong simplifying assumptions:

- Linear impact functions.

- Simple price dynamics (e.g., Brownian motion with constant volatility).
- No microstructure frictions.
- Continuous control over deterministic trade sizes.

Once we view execution as an MDP, we open the door to RL methods:

- The *policy* is a mapping from current state (remaining inventory, time, market conditions) to actions (trade size and style).
- Instead of solving for a fixed curve at time 0, an RL agent learns a policy that adapts at each step to the realized market conditions.
- The classical optimal schedule can serve as an anchor: it defines what a reasonable risk-impact trade-off looks like in an idealized world. RL generalizes this to more realistic, high-dimensional, and partially observable settings.

RL Policies as Data-Driven Schedulers

An RL-based execution algorithm can be thought of as a *data-driven scheduler*. It keeps many of the conceptual features of classical optimal execution while relaxing their rigid assumptions.

Inherited structure. The agent still:

- Tracks remaining inventory and time.
- Trades off impact against risk.
- Respects participation caps and other constraints (imposed via the action space or rule-based overrides).

Additional flexibility. Beyond the classical model, RL allows the policy to:

- Condition on rich, non-linear features of the limit order book (spread, depth imbalance, queue sizes).

- Adapt to changing volatility in real time rather than using a constant σ.
- Learn impact and resilience patterns directly from historical data, rather than fixing them to linear forms.
- Incorporate more complex objectives, such as outperforming VWAP while limiting the variance of implementation shortfall.

Risk-impact trade-off in RL. The same risk-impact trade-off reappears in RL design:

- The *reward function* encodes how we penalize impact costs and risk (for example, penalizing large inventory late in the horizon).
- The *policy constraints* (e.g., caps on participation rates) and regularizers prevent the agent from overfitting to rare events or pursuing fragile, overly aggressive tactics.

From this perspective, classical optimal execution is not replaced by RL; instead, it provides:

- Intuition about sensible behavior (e.g., trade faster in high volatility).
- Baseline schedules for comparison in backtests.
- Structural guidance for state variables, constraints, and reward design.

In the next section, we will make the MDP formulation more explicit at the microstructure level, defining states, actions, and rewards when the environment is a limit order book, and showing how RL policies can control both *when* to trade and *how* to place orders across multiple venues.

5.2 RL for Adaptive Order Placement and Routing

In the previous section we treated execution primarily as a *scheduling* problem: how to spread a parent order over time to balance expected market impact and price risk. The resulting optimal schedule was a curve of target inventories, computed in advance under a stylized model of price dynamics and impact.

Real execution, however, happens at the level of concrete orders interacting with a limit order book (LOB). At each moment you must choose:

- *Order type*: market, limit, immediate-or-cancel (IOC), pegged, hidden, etc.
- *Price*: at the touch, inside the spread, or deeper in the book.
- *Size*: how many shares to send now versus later.
- *Venue*: which exchange or dark pool to use when there are multiple choices.

These decisions must be made repeatedly, under uncertainty, using an imperfect and delayed view of the order book. This is exactly the setting where reinforcement learning becomes powerful. In this section we formalize smart execution as a Markov Decision Process (MDP) and then as a Partially Observable MDP (POMDP), and we describe how RL agents can use noisy LOB information and impact forecasts to learn adaptive order-placement and routing policies.

From Schedules to Microstructure Decisions

The optimal execution schedule gives you a *time-profile of desired trading*. For example, you might want to buy 30% of the order in the next ten minutes, 20% in the following ten, and so on. But the schedule does not tell you *how* to achieve those targets in the LOB.

There is a second layer of decisions:

- **Scheduling layer**: how fast should my remaining inventory decline as a function of time and market conditions?
- **Placement and routing layer**: given a desired trading intensity right now, how should I express this demand as actual orders across venues and order types?

Classical models largely abstract away from the placement layer by assuming you can trade a quantity at the model's "execution price." In reality, you must choose between, say:

- Hitting the best offer with a market order (fast execution, but you cross the spread and risk impact).
- Posting a passive limit buy order at or below the best bid (cheaper if you get filled, but risk of non-execution or adverse selection).
- Splitting the size across several venues or dark pools.

These choices are path-dependent and interact with latent liquidity, other participants' behavior, and your own previous actions. This motivates moving from a static schedule to a sequential decision framework.

Execution as a Markov Decision Process

We start with the idealized case where the agent's state representation captures the relevant information to make good decisions; later we will relax this to partial observability.

An MDP is defined by:

- A set of states S.
- A set of actions A.
- A transition mechanism describing how states evolve given actions.
- A reward signal r received at each step.

State: What the Agent Knows

For smart execution, a natural state at decision time t_k combines:

Inventory and clock.

- Remaining inventory x_k for the parent order.
- Time-to-deadline τ_k (e.g., minutes or decision steps left until the order must be complete).

These variables ensure the agent knows its urgency: a large remaining inventory with little time left should induce more aggressive actions.

Limit order book features.

The full LOB is high-dimensional: many price levels on each side, quantities at each level, and dynamic queues. For RL, we typically work with a summarized but informative view, for example:

- Best bid and best ask prices; current spread.
- Depth at the first few levels of bid and ask (e.g., aggregated volume at top 5 levels).
- Order book imbalance (difference between bid and ask depth).
- Recent trade prices and sizes (e.g., last n trades).
- Short-term volatility and realized spread.

These features tell the agent whether the market is currently tight or wide, liquid or thin, and whether there is buying or selling pressure.

Constraints and context.

- Participation cap: current estimate of total market volume and how much the agent is already participating.
- Venue-specific information: which venues are available, their historical fill rates, and fee/rebate structures.
- Any internal risk limits or execution style preferences (e.g., "do not cross more than X% of the spread on average").

The state vector thus concatenates execution variables (inventory, time), microstructure variables (LOB snapshot, recent trades), and constraint variables (caps, venue flags).

Action: How the Agent Trades

An action must capture the key placement and routing degrees of freedom. A pragmatic design is to define the action as a structured object with several components:

- **Order type**: discrete choice among {market, limit, IOC, hidden, pegged}.
- **Aggressiveness or price offset**: for a buy order, this might be "post at best bid," "join the bid-1 tick," "cross the spread by one tick," etc. We can encode this as a discrete number of ticks relative to the best prices.
- **Slice size**: fraction of remaining inventory to trade now, or absolute number of shares, possibly bounded by participation caps.
- **Venue or pool**: discrete choice over exchanges and dark pools.

We can treat the joint action as either:

- A single high-dimensional discrete action (e.g., a catalog of allowed combinations of type, price offset, size bucket, and venue), or
- A factored action where an RL policy has multiple output heads: one for type, one for price offset, one for size, one for venue.

The second option is often easier to scale and interpret; it also aligns well with hierarchical policies where scheduling and placement are partially separated.

Transition: What Happens After an Action

Once an action is taken, the environment:

- Processes the order(s) according to exchange matching rules.
- Realizes fills based on current and future order flow.
- Updates the mid-price, spread, and depths.
- Advances time and updates remaining inventory based on filled quantities.

From the agent's perspective, these transitions are stochastic: the same action in the same apparent state might yield different fills and price paths depending on random order flow from other participants.

Reward: Measuring Execution Performance

The reward should reflect progress on the execution objective. A common choice is to connect directly to implementation shortfall. For a buy order, a simple per-step reward at decision time t_k can be:

- Negative of the cost incurred by any fills in the interval, measured relative to the arrival price P_0 or an evolving benchmark such as VWAP.
- Additional penalty for having large remaining inventory late in the horizon, to encode risk aversion and deadlines.
- Optionally, penalties for undesirable behavior (e.g., repeatedly flashing large orders that get canceled, which could signal information).

For example, you may define

$$r_k = -\sum_{\text{fills in } k} (P_{fill} - P_{bench}) \cdot q_{fill} - \alpha \cdot \big(\text{inventory risk term at } k\big),$$

where α controls risk sensitivity. The cumulative reward over the episode is then (minus) implementation shortfall plus risk adjustments.

Why Partial Observability Matters

The MDP description above implicitly assumes that the state vector contains all the information needed to make optimal decisions. In reality, the agent never sees:

- Hidden orders (e.g., iceberg or fully hidden liquidity).
- Private intentions of other traders.
- Future order arrivals and cancellations.
- The true impact function: how others will react to your order.

Moreover, due to latency and data processing delays, even the visible part of the LOB is slightly stale by the time you act on it. This makes the problem naturally *partially observable*. A more faithful model is therefore a POMDP:

- **Hidden state** z_k: the true, full market state, including all resting and incoming orders, hidden liquidity, and other participants' decision rules.
- **Observation** o_k: what the agent actually sees - a noisy, delayed LOB snapshot, recent trades, and its own inventory/time.
- **Action** a_k: the order placement and routing decision, as before.
- **Reward** r_k: realized cost/reward from fills, as before.

The agent does not directly observe z_k and must therefore form an *internal belief* about the underlying market conditions. This can be done in two broad ways:

- **Explicit belief models**: maintain a parametric or particle-based belief distribution over hidden variables such as latent liquidity or short-term drift, and update it using Bayesian filtering as new observations arrive. This can be statistically appealing but is often complex in high dimensions.

- **Implicit memory via recurrent networks**: feed sequences of observations and actions into a recurrent neural network (e.g., LSTM or GRU). The hidden state of the network acts as a compressed summary of recent history, capturing patterns in order flow that help infer latent conditions.

In practice, RL for execution often uses the second approach: the policy $\pi_\theta(a_k \mid h_k)$ depends on a hidden representation h_k that is updated with each new observation and action.

A POMDP View of Smart Execution

We can now summarize smart execution as a POMDP:

- At each decision step k, the environment reveals an observation o_k (LOB snapshot, remaining inventory, time).
- The agent updates its internal memory h_k based on (h_{k-1}, o_k).
- The agent samples an action a_k from its policy $\pi(a_k \mid h_k)$: select order type, price offset, size, and venue.
- The environment processes the orders, produces fills and a new underlying state z_{k+1}, and returns a reward r_k plus a new observation o_{k+1}.

The goal of the agent is to choose a policy that maximizes the expected sum of rewards over the life of the order, which corresponds to minimizing expected execution cost (and possibly its risk).

Right after formalizing this POMDP, it is useful to give the reader a visual map of the loop.

This diagram highlights the core loop: observations from a LOB environment flow into an RL agent, which outputs actions (orders) that affect the environment and generate rewards based on implementation shortfall and risk.

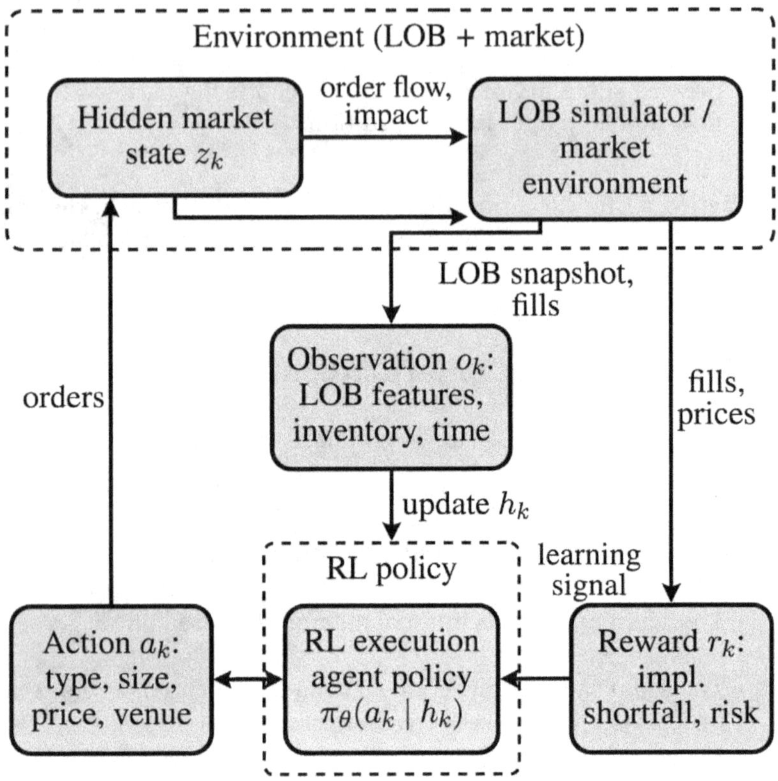

Designing State and Action Spaces

The quality of an RL execution agent depends heavily on how we formulate the state and action spaces. Poor design can make learning impossible or lead to policies that exploit unrealistic artifacts of the simulator.

State considerations

When building the state representation, practitioners balance three goals:

- **Expressiveness**: the state should contain enough information to approximate an optimal policy.
- **Compactness**: overly large state spaces slow learning and increase overfitting risk.
- **Robustness**: state variables should be stable and not overly sensitive to noise or specific microstructure features that will change over time.

Typical design choices include:

- Using relative prices (e.g., normalized by arrival price or a recent mid-price) rather than raw prices.
- Including short histories (e.g., a few past LOB snapshots and trades) to help the agent infer trends and resiliency.
- Encoding inventory and time in normalized units (e.g., remaining inventory as a fraction of the initial order, time as fraction of total horizon).

Action granularity

On the action side, there is a similar tension:

- **Fine-grained actions**: allow the agent to choose arbitrary sizes and precise price offsets. This can, in theory, uncover subtle patterns but greatly expands the action space.
- **Coarse-grained actions**: restrict the agent to a small set of intuitive tactics, like "aggressive buy," "passive buy," "post hidden order," or "route to dark pool." This simplifies learning and improves interpretability but may leave some performance on the table.

A practical compromise is to discretize size and aggressiveness:

- Sizes: small / medium / large, defined as fractions of remaining inventory or participation caps.

- Aggressiveness: e.g., post at bid, cross by one tick, cross by two ticks.

Such discretization also makes it easier to map RL actions into real order-entry messages and to implement rule-based safeguards (e.g., "never choose the most aggressive action more than X times in a row").

Training Regimes: Offline and Online

Given a POMDP formulation and a choice of state and action spaces, the next question is how to train the RL policy.

Offline RL from historical data

The safest starting point is *offline* (or batch) RL:

- Collect historical LOB data and order/quote messages.
- Simulate how a reference policy (e.g., an existing execution algorithm) would have traded, or use actual historical executions.
- Learn a policy that would have improved execution, given these past trajectories, without live experimentation.

Offline RL must address distribution shift: the data come from a behavior policy that may differ from the new policy being learned. Algorithms such as conservative Q-learning or implicit behavioral cloning regularize the learned policy toward actions that appear sufficiently often in the data, reducing the risk of extrapolating to unsupported regions of the state-action space.

Online fine-tuning in a simulator

To go beyond what offline data can reliably identify, we can fine-tune the policy *online* in a high-fidelity LOB simulator:

- The simulator replays or synthetically generates order flow and enforces exchange matching rules.

- The policy interacts with this environment, trying new actions and observing the resulting rewards.
- Standard RL algorithms (e.g., policy gradient, actor-critic) can then be used without the off-policy complications of offline data.

This closed-loop training allows the agent to discover creative placements and routings. However, it is only as good as the simulator; overfitting to simulator quirks is a real danger and will be addressed more fully in the section on microstructure-aware simulation and sim-to-real transfer.

Safety mechanisms and constraints

Regardless of training paradigm, execution RL must respect safety constraints:

- **Action clipping**: enforce hard limits on order size, aggressiveness, and participation rates.
- **Rule-based overrides**: allow risk managers to override or veto certain actions (e.g., during extreme volatility or halts).
- **Circuit breakers**: automatically fall back to a conservative baseline algorithm (e.g., a VWAP-style strategy) if the RL agent's behavior or performance deviates beyond predefined thresholds.

From an RL perspective, these controls effectively restrict the action space - the policy can recommend any action, but only those passing the filters are executed.

Illustrative Behavior of an RL Execution Policy

To make the abstract formulation more concrete, consider how a well-trained RL agent might behave in simple scenarios.

Scenario 1: Tight spread, deep book, low volatility.

- The LOB shows large depth at the best bid and ask and a very small spread.

- The agent has moderate time left and a moderate inventory.
- The agent might choose relatively passive limit orders near the best bid, occasionally crossing by one tick when it detects that the queue ahead is too long.
- It may also route to venues with lower fees or higher historical fill rates, even if the visible quotes look similar.

Scenario 2: Widening spread, thinning depth, volatility spike.

- The spread has widened, depth is low, and recent trades show rapid price changes.
- The agent still has significant inventory left but less time.
- A risk-aware RL policy, influenced by its reward design, might accept higher impact costs and use more market or aggressive limit orders to ensure completion, particularly on venues that historically absorb shocks better.
- If volatility remains high but depth recovers, the agent may revert to slightly less aggressive tactics, showing nuanced adaptation instead of a fixed rule like "always trade faster in high volatility."

Scenario 3: Hidden liquidity in dark pools.

- The visible LOB is thin, but the agent's recurrent state has learned that, in similar conditions and at this time of day, sending small probing orders to certain dark pools often results in favorable midpoint fills.
- The agent intermittently routes small IOC or hidden orders to those venues before crossing lit markets, balancing the chance of cheap fills against the risk of delay.

In each case, the RL agent is effectively implementing a *data-driven scheduling and placement policy* that responds to evolving market features. It generalizes the classical notion of an optimal schedule by embedding it in a richer, microstructure-aware, sequential decision framework.

In this section we lifted execution from a static, curve-based scheduling model to a dynamic, microstructure-level reinforcement learning problem. We:

- Formulated smart execution as an MDP and then as a POMDP, highlighting the role of partial observability and latent liquidity.
- Described state and action spaces that allow an RL agent to decide order type, size, timing, and venue based on noisy LOB states and impact considerations.
- Connected the reward design to implementation shortfall and risk aversion, mirroring the trade-offs in classical optimal execution.
- Outlined training regimes (offline and online in simulators) and safety constraints that make RL-based execution practical.

The next sections will deepen the discussion along two axes: the infrastructural realities that affect observations and fills (latency and slippage attribution), and the construction of realistic LOB simulators that enable robust training and safe transfer of RL policies to live markets.

5.3 Latency, Infrastructure, and Slippage Attribution

Up to this point we have treated the execution environment as if orders and information flowed instantaneously. The optimal schedule and RL policies operated on a limit order book whose state was assumed to be current, and fills were assumed to happen "now" at prices determined by simple impact models.

In real markets, this picture is too clean. Every action and observation is delayed by the plumbing of the system: networks, switches, matching engines, and clocks. These delays are often measured in microseconds or milliseconds, but at modern trading speeds they are economically significant. An RL execution policy that ignores latency and infrastructure will misjudge the true state of the book and the true cause of its slippage.

In this section we:

- Decompose implementation shortfall into components that can be linked to infrastructure.
- Describe the main sources of latency and how they distort the RL agent's perception of the environment.
- Explain how to build latency-aware RL environments and reward signals.
- Discuss slippage attribution techniques that separate market, algorithmic, and infrastructural effects.
- Outline design principles for RL policies that remain robust under latency and fill uncertainty.

From Total Shortfall to a Cost Stack

Recall that *implementation shortfall* measures the difference between the actual execution value and the value at the decision (arrival) price. For a buy order of size Q, with arrival mid-price P_0 and realized average execution price P_{exec}, the shortfall is:

$$\text{IS} = Q \cdot (P_{exec} - P_0),$$

where a positive number means worse performance than the arrival price.

To understand *why* this shortfall arises, practitioners mentally (and often quantitatively) break it into layers:

1. **Market drift**: the price move that would have happened even if you did nothing.
2. **Spread costs**: the cost of crossing the bid-ask spread with market or aggressively priced limits.

3. **Market impact**: the price move caused by your own trading (both temporary and permanent).
4. **Latency-induced slippage**: additional cost from acting on stale information or having orders arrive too late or too early relative to the current market.
5. **Residual and modeling error**: everything else, including noise and mis-estimation of the first three components.

Classical optimal execution frameworks focus mostly on spread and impact, treating drift as exogenous. Latency and infrastructure sit in the fourth component, but they also interact with the others: for example, delayed market data can cause a policy to underestimate the spread or overestimate available depth, which in turn leads to more impact and spread cost.

For RL to learn sensible behavior, the environment must reflect these layers, and the reward signals must make it possible to attribute which part of the shortfall stems from the policy versus from the infrastructure.

Sources and Types of Latency

Latency is the time between an event happening in the market and that event being visible or actionable by the agent. It is more useful to think of latency as a chain of intervals rather than a single number.

Market data latency

This is the delay between an exchange matching an order (e.g., a trade occurs, the best bid moves) and the agent seeing this change in its incoming data:

- The exchange's matching engine updates its internal state.
- The exchange's feed handler packages the changes into multicast messages and sends them out.
- These packets travel over physical links (fiber, microwave) to the trading firm's data center.

- The firm's own feed handlers parse, normalize, and distribute the messages to the RL agent.

By the time the agent observes a LOB snapshot, it is already slightly out of date. In calm markets, this staleness may be negligible; in fast markets, it can be the difference between hitting a displayed quote and trading through several levels worse.

Order-entry and acknowledgment latency

Similarly, when the RL agent decides to send an order:

- The order message must travel from the agent process to the firm's order gateway.
- It is then transmitted to the exchange's gateway and forwarded to the matching engine.
- The matching engine processes the order (possibly queuing it) and sends back acknowledgments and fills.

The time from decision to *effective arrival* of the order at the matching engine is the *decision-to-book latency*. This delay means that when the agent chooses a price and size, it is doing so assuming a book that may already have changed by the time the order is eligible to interact with it.

Queuing latency

Even after the order reaches the book, it may not execute immediately:

- A passive limit order will rest in a price-level queue; it is filled only after earlier orders at that price are executed or canceled.
- Queue length and cancellation behavior of other participants determine the waiting time.

This queuing delay is another form of latency between "intent to trade" and "actual execution," and it is affected by both microstructure and your own order-placement strategy.

Jitter and variability

None of these latencies are constant. They fluctuate due to:

- Network congestion and routing changes.
- Load on exchange systems and your own infrastructure.
- Operating system scheduling and application-level load.

The variability itself matters: an RL agent might adapt to a fixed, known delay, but random jitter makes timing less predictable and increases uncertainty about fills.

Infrastructure Building Blocks

To make latency more concrete, it helps to outline the main hardware and software components between RL policy and exchange:

- **Co-location and data centers**: firms often place servers physically near exchange matching engines to reduce path length and variability.
- **Feed handlers**: processes that receive exchange multicast feeds, decode binary messages, and construct LOB snapshots or event streams.
- **Order gateways and risk checks**: systems that accept orders from strategies, apply pre-trade risk limits (size checks, credit limits), and forward them to exchanges.
- **Clock synchronization**: protocols such as PTP (Precision Time Protocol) are used to keep timestamps consistent across machines so that event timing can be reconstructed accurately.

For human traders, many of these details are invisible. For an RL agent, they define what the state actually means: a "current" LOB snapshot is in fact a view of the book as it was a few hundred microseconds or milliseconds ago, with timestamping accuracy that depends on clock synchronization quality.

How Latency Distorts the RL Environment

From the perspective of the RL formulation, latency turns a clean MDP into a more challenging POMDP with delayed actions:

- Observations o_k do not correspond exactly to the true state z_k at decision time but to $z_{k-\delta^o}$, where δ^o represents data latency.
- Actions a_k affect the environment not immediately but after a delay δ^a, during which the state may have evolved substantially.
- Rewards r_k corresponding to a given action may arrive several steps later, once fills are confirmed and priced.

If the environment simulator ignores these effects, the RL agent will implicitly learn a policy that relies on being able to react to instantaneous information and to have orders take effect immediately. When deployed in a real infrastructure, such a policy can behave pathologically:

- Overestimating fill probabilities for passive orders, because in reality the displayed depth was consumed before the order arrived.
- Underestimating the risk of crossing the spread just as the market moves, leading to frequent "last look" style adverse fills.
- Exploiting unrealistically precise timing in the simulator (e.g., always canceling just before being hit), which is impossible with real jitter.

To avoid this, we must embed latency into both the state and the transition dynamics of the RL environment.

Latency-Aware RL Environment Design

Building a latency-aware execution environment involves three main steps.

Timestamp everything

The foundation is accurate timekeeping:

- Market data messages from exchanges carry exchange timestamps.
- Internal components (feed handlers, gateways, RL agent) add their own local timestamps when events are processed.
- Clock synchronization protocols align these clocks to a common reference so differences between timestamps can be interpreted.

In the simulator, these timestamps define:

- When a particular LOB snapshot becomes visible to the agent.
- When an action is decided and at what simulated time it reaches the book.
- When fills occur and when they are reported back to the agent.

Model decision-to-book and data delays

In a microstructure-aware simulator:

- An observation at simulated time t is generated from the LOB state at $t - \delta^o$, where δ^o can be fixed or sampled from an empirical distribution of data latencies.
- When the agent acts at time t, the order is queued to arrive at the matching engine at $t + \delta^a$, again possibly sampled from a realistic distribution.
- If the simulator replays historical data, the recorded event timestamps and a model of your own historical path can be used to calibrate these delays.

This ensures the agent trains on the *effective* environment it will face in production, not an idealized instantaneous one.

Handle delayed and sparse rewards

Because fills can be delayed, the RL environment must be explicit about which rewards correspond to which actions:

- One approach is to accumulate all fill-related costs in a buffer and assign them to the time step at which they are observed by the agent. This keeps the MDP structure but introduces noisy credit assignment.
- A more refined approach is to attribute fills back to the decision that created the corresponding order, effectively creating a semi-MDP with options. This can improve learning but is more complex to implement.

In either case, the agent must cope with the fact that the immediate reward after an action may not fully reflect the long-term cost of that decision. This pushes us toward algorithms and architectures that handle delayed rewards gracefully, such as recurrent actor-critic methods.

Slippage Attribution: Market vs. Algorithm vs. Infrastructure

Once latency is modeled, we can better answer a key question: when the RL execution policy underperforms, is it because the market moved unexpectedly, because the policy made poor decisions, or because the infrastructure was slow?

A practical slippage attribution framework might proceed in layers:

1. Structural market component

- Compute how much of the price move would have occurred even with a “do nothing” strategy, using a neutral benchmark like VWAP or mid-price drift over the trading horizon.
- This captures unavoidable market risk given the trade horizon and size.

2. Algorithmic component

- Compare the RL policy’s performance to that of a reference algorithm (e.g., a well-calibrated VWAP or optimal schedule) operating under the *same* latency model.

- Differences reflect how well the RL agent chooses order types, sizes, and venues given the same infrastructure constraints.

3. Infrastructural component

- Simulate the RL policy under an ideal, low-latency environment and compare to its performance under the real latency profile.
- The gap isolates the cost of delays and jitter, given a fixed policy.
- Further break down this gap by source: market data delay vs. order-entry delay vs. queuing, using controlled experiments (e.g., artificially increasing one component at a time in the simulator).

The resulting "cost stack" allows teams to see, for example, that 60% of total shortfall is structural (market drift), 25% is attributable to policy decisions (e.g., systematically too passive late in the schedule), and 15% comes from infrastructure (e.g., a congested network path at peak times). This, in turn, guides whether to prioritize policy improvements, infrastructure investment, or adjustments to trading objectives.

Designing Latency-Robust RL Policies

Beyond modeling latency in the environment, we can actively encourage the RL policy to be robust to timing uncertainty.

Train with latency randomization

Instead of a fixed latency, expose the agent during training to a range of plausible delays and jitter patterns:

- Sample δ^o and δ^a at each episode (or even each step) from calibrated distributions.
- Vary queuing behavior by sampling cancellation rates and order flow intensities.

This is a form of domain randomization: the agent learns a policy that performs well across a family of environments rather than exploiting a single, precise timing pattern.

Favor strategies that are less timing-sensitive

Within the action space and reward design, we can steer the policy away from brittle tactics that depend on microsecond-level precision:

- Penalize excessive order cancellations or rapid "pinging" of the book, which are often sensitive to exact latency.
- Encourage more robust placement strategies, such as using slightly more conservative price levels instead of trying to snipe fleeting quotes.
- Incorporate a small penalty on the variance of realized execution prices, discouraging policies that rely on rare, perfectly-timed favorable fills.

These signals guide the RL algorithm toward strategies that are smoother and easier to implement in real infrastructure.

Use conservative baselines and fallbacks

As discussed previously, execution RL should be wrapped in safety mechanisms:

- If monitoring detects that actual latencies have drifted outside the range seen during training (e.g., due to a network failure), automatically reduce the policy's aggressiveness or fall back to a simpler baseline algorithm.
- Incorporate "latency features" (e.g., recent round-trip times or observed book update rates) into the state, so the agent can adapt its behavior when the infrastructure slows down.

An RL policy that is explicitly aware of and trained over varying latencies is better equipped to remain stable under operational stress.

Implications for Evaluation and Deployment

Latency and infrastructure complicate not just training but also evaluation and live rollout.

Backtesting with latency

When backtesting RL policies on historical data:

- You must reconstruct not only the sequence of market events but also the timing of when they would have been visible to the strategy, given realistic feed delays.
- Similarly, you must simulate when orders would have reached the book and how they would have interacted with the historical order flow.

Ignoring these factors leads to overly optimistic backtest results and policies that may fail catastrophically in production.

A/B testing and slippage monitoring

In live deployment:

- Run RL policies in parallel with existing algorithms under comparable latency conditions, and compare performance using the layered slippage attribution described above.
- Continuously monitor latency metrics (e.g., distribution of decision-to-book times, data arrival times) alongside execution metrics, so that degradations in infrastructure can be distinguished from policy failures.

This holistic view is crucial when deciding whether an RL policy is truly adding value or simply trading under more favorable infrastructural conditions.

Latency and infrastructure turn the theoretically clean RL execution problem into a richer and more challenging POMDP with delayed and noisy observations and actions. In this section we:

- Decomposed implementation shortfall into components, highlighting where latency-induced slippage fits.
- Surveyed market data, order-entry, and queuing latencies and discussed how they arise from real infrastructure.

- Explained how ignoring latency distorts the RL environment and leads to fragile policies.
- Outlined how to build latency-aware simulators with proper timestamping, delayed observations/actions, and delayed rewards.
- Presented slippage attribution techniques to separate market, algorithmic, and infrastructural contributions to costs.
- Proposed training and design strategies to make RL policies robust under timing uncertainty.

With these elements in place, we can now turn to the construction of microstructure-aware simulators and the challenge of transferring RL execution policies safely from simulation to live markets.

5.4 Microstructure-Aware Simulation and Transfer to Live

The previous sections treated the limit order book (LOB) as a given environment whose imperfections—latency, partial observability, and impact—an RL agent must learn to navigate. In practice, before we ever allow an RL policy to touch real capital, we need a *safe* environment in which the agent can explore, make mistakes, and improve. That environment is almost always a simulator.

In this section we focus on two intertwined questions:

- How do we build a LOB simulator that is realistic enough for training execution policies?
- How do we transfer policies trained in such simulators into live markets without being surprised by the inevitable discrepancies?

We will move step by step from basic microstructure mechanics to full simulation and then to deployment patterns that connect simulation and reality.

Why Microstructure Detail Matters for RL

For many classical execution models, a coarse representation of the market—mid-prices, spreads, average volume—is sufficient. RL for order placement and routing, however, acts at the microsecond-to-second scale and interacts directly with the order book. Its behavior depends critically on:

- Queue positions and cancellations.
- How quickly impact decays (order book resiliency).
- Hidden liquidity and dark-pool fill probabilities.
- Latency variations and message-level workflows.

If the simulator does not reflect these features reasonably well, the RL agent may discover strategies that perform spectacularly in sim but fail badly live. Common failure modes include:

- Exploiting unrealistic arbitrage or timing opportunities that do not exist in real markets.
- Relying on overly optimistic fill rates or depth that vanish in production.
- Learning to "game" simulator-specific bugs or simplifications.

A microstructure-aware simulator aims to capture enough of the market's structure and randomness to discourage such brittle strategies while remaining tractable to build and calibrate.

Building Blocks of a LOB Simulator

A limit order book simulator represents a matching engine and the surrounding order flow. At a high level, it must model:

- The **order types** that participants can send.

- The **priority rules** that determine how orders are queued and matched.
- The **event flow** of incoming orders, trades, and cancellations.
- The **price impact and resiliency** resulting from trades.

Order types and matching rules

At minimum, the simulator should implement:

- *Limit orders*: rest in the book until filled or canceled.
- *Market orders*: execute immediately against the best available opposite-side liquidity.
- *Immediate-or-cancel (IOC)* and *fill-or-kill (FOK)* variants.
- Basic support for pegged or hidden orders if your strategy will use them.

Matching rules specify:

- **Price-time priority** (or other variants such as pro-rata).
- Handling of partial fills and residual quantities.
- Auction mechanisms (opening/closing auctions), if relevant to your trading horizon.

Implementing these correctly is more important than making them lightning fast; RL training can tolerate some simulation overhead, but systematic discrepancies in matching logic will mislead the agent.

Event-driven vs. snapshot-based simulation

There are two common approaches to driving the simulator:

1. Event-driven simulation. The environment processes a chronological sequence of events (limit order arrivals, market orders, cancellations, etc.). Each event updates the book state and may generate fills for the agent's orders.

- Pros: naturally mirrors exchange message streams; fine-grained control over timing.
- Cons: requires high-quality event data or a realistic event generator.

2. Snapshot-based simulation. The environment uses a time series of aggregate book states (e.g., every 100 ms). Agent actions are applied between snapshots, and fills are simulated based on depth changes and modeled order flow.

- Pros: easier to implement when only snapshots are available; lower data volume.
- Cons: coarser timing; must infer or approximate the unseen micro-events between snapshots.

For execution RL, where timing and queue dynamics are important, an event-driven simulator is preferable when possible. Snapshot-based approaches can still be useful in lower-frequency regimes or for early prototyping.

Order flow: replay vs. synthetic generation

The heart of the simulator is the background order flow from other market participants. There are three main strategies:

Historical replay.

- Use recorded exchange feeds to reconstruct the exact sequence of public orders, trades, and cancellations.
- Insert the agent's orders into this flow and match them as if the agent had traded in that historical period.

This gives maximal realism for visible liquidity, but it cannot account for the fact that in reality, your orders would slightly change other participants' behavior and prices. For moderate participation rates, this is often acceptable.

Parametric order-flow models.

- Model order arrivals as stochastic processes (e.g., Poisson or Hawkes processes) with parameters calibrated to historical data.
- Generate synthetic streams of orders and cancellations that reproduce key statistics such as spreads, depth distributions, and trade intensities.

This increases scenario diversity and allows you to generate long simulations under varying conditions, but realism depends heavily on model choice and calibration quality.

Learned generative models.

- Use machine learning models (e.g., recurrent networks, variational autoencoders, generative adversarial networks) trained on historical order flow to produce realistic synthetic streams.
- These can capture complex temporal dependencies and regime changes that are hard to specify parametrically.

This approach is powerful but still an active research area; quality assessment and control are non-trivial. For production RL training, many firms prefer simpler, more interpretable generative models backed by sanity checks.

In practice, a hybrid approach is common: historical replay for baseline realism, augmented with parametric or learned models for stress scenarios or rare regimes underrepresented in historical data.

Calibrating the Simulator to Market Data

A simulator is only as good as its calibration. Calibration aligns the simulator's behavior with stylized facts and statistics observed in real markets.

Stylized microstructure facts

Before tuning any RL agent, ensure the simulator reproduces key features such as:

- **Spread distribution**: how often the spread is at one tick, two ticks, etc.

- **Depth profiles**: typical volume at the best bid/ask and a few levels deeper.
- **Volatility and return distribution**: intraday volatility patterns, heavy tails.
- **Order sign and size statistics**: distribution of buy vs. sell market orders, size distributions, and clustering.
- **Resiliency**: how quickly the book refills after a large trade; impact decay.

If the simulator does not match these broad characteristics, RL agents will learn behaviors that exploit unrealistic patterns (e.g., always expecting the spread to revert in one step) and will not transfer well.

Impact and resiliency modeling

To support execution RL, the simulator must capture how your own trades move the market:

- Temporary impact: immediate widening of the spread or depletion of depth when your large orders hit the book.
- Permanent impact: persistent shifts in mid-price following sustained buying or selling pressure.
- Resiliency: how quickly order book depth and spreads revert to normal after your trade.

You can calibrate impact by analyzing historical trades that are plausibly exogenous and measuring subsequent price paths. Simple linear or square-root models for impact can then be embedded into the simulator, possibly conditioned on volatility and liquidity regimes.

Latency and infrastructure calibration

As discussed in the previous section, realistic modeling of latency is crucial. Use production telemetry (timestamps from feed handlers, gateways, and exchanges) to estimate:

- Distributions of market data delays from exchange to your systems.

- Distributions of order-entry and acknowledgment delays.
- Typical queuing times at various participation rates and price levels.

These distributions can be used to inject realistic delays into the simulator, ensuring RL agents experience the same "staleness" and variability they will see in production.

Domain Randomization and Ensemble Environments

Even a carefully calibrated simulator cannot perfectly match live markets. One of the most effective ways to make RL policies robust to this mismatch is to train them across *families* of simulated environments instead of a single "best guess."

Domain randomization

Domain randomization means that on each training episode, you randomize some of the environment's parameters within plausible ranges, for example:

- Volatility levels and intraday volatility patterns.
- Average spread and depth.
- Impact coefficients and resiliency speeds.
- Latency distributions and jitter magnitudes.
- Order-flow intensities and buy/sell imbalances.

The RL agent must learn a policy that performs well across these varied conditions, rather than over-optimizing for one particular setting. This encourages strategies that are adaptive and conservative: they work reasonably well even when the simulator is slightly wrong.

Ensemble of scenarios

In addition to randomization, you can define a discrete ensemble of representative scenarios:

- Calm, liquid market (tight spreads, deep books, low volatility).
- Volatile yet liquid market (tight spreads but high volatility).
- Illiquid market (wide spreads, thin depth).
- Stress regimes (extreme volatility, rapidly changing order flow).

Each training episode samples one scenario, and performance metrics are tracked per-scenario. This allows you to diagnose whether the policy is robust across regimes and to introduce scenario-specific reward shaping if needed (e.g., higher risk aversion in stress scenarios).

Conservative RL Objectives for Execution

When training in simulated environments, it is tempting to chase maximal expected reward. However, small model errors can lead agents to adopt fragile policies. To mitigate this, we can design *conservative* RL objectives:

- **Risk-sensitive rewards**: penalize not just average implementation shortfall but also its variance or downside tail. For example, add a penalty proportional to the variance of per-episode shortfall across scenarios.
- **Regularization toward baselines**: encourage the policy to stay close to a well-understood heuristic (e.g., VWAP or classical optimal schedule) unless strong evidence suggests deviating. This can be done via KL-penalties between the RL policy and a baseline policy.
- **Constraint-aware learning**: explicitly encode participation caps, maximum aggression, and inventory-risk limits into the action space and reward. Policies that violate these constraints in sim will be discouraged, reducing the risk of dangerous behavior in live trading.

These techniques aim to produce policies that may sacrifice a small amount of expected performance in-sim in exchange for robustness and safety under inevitable model imperfections.

From Simulator to Production: Staged Deployment

Even with careful design and conservative training objectives, a simulator cannot substitute fully for live experience. A cautious, staged deployment path bridges the gap.

Shadow mode

In *shadow mode*, the RL policy runs live in parallel with existing execution algorithms but does not control any orders:

- For each real parent order, the RL policy receives the same market data and internal state as the production algorithm.
- It outputs hypothetical actions; these are recorded but not sent to the market.
- A simulator or "paper trader" uses live market data to compute the hypothetical fills and P&L that the RL policy would have achieved.

Shadow mode enables apples-to-apples comparison between RL and existing algorithms under real conditions, including true latency, without risking capital. It also generates valuable off-policy data for further training and debugging.

Limited live rollout and A/B testing

Once shadow results are satisfactory and risk managers are comfortable, the next step is limited live deployment:

- Assign a small fraction of eligible orders (e.g., 1–5%) to the RL policy; the rest continue to use legacy algorithms.
- Use A/B testing to compare execution quality, slippage components, and risk metrics between RL and control groups.
- Maintain tight risk limits: caps on maximum participation, maximum order size per child order, and total daily exposure.

Feedback from this phase refines both the policy and the simulator: discrepancies between simulated and realized performance highlight gaps in modeling or calibration.

Incremental scaling and continuous monitoring

If limited deployment is successful, gradually increase RL's share of order flow, while continuously monitoring:

- Implementation shortfall and its decomposition (market vs. algorithmic vs. infrastructure).
- Behavior metrics: aggression levels, cancellation rates, venue usage patterns.
- Stability under market regime changes (e.g., earnings days, macro announcements).

A robust monitoring framework should include automated alerts and fail-safes that revert to conservative baselines if performance drifts or if environment conditions (e.g., latency) move outside the range seen during training.

Closing the Loop: Updating Simulator and Policy

Deployment is not the end of the story. Markets evolve, and so must both the simulator and the RL policy.

Simulator updates from live data

Live trading generates rich data beyond what historical tapes capture:

- Your own impact patterns under the current style and volume.
- Actual fill probabilities for different order types on different venues, conditional on current market conditions.
- Realized latency and jitter distributions as infrastructure or exchange behavior changes.

Regularly feeding these observations back into the simulator—updating order-flow parameters, impact coefficients, latency models, and scenario distributions—keeps it aligned with the current market.

Policy adaptation and retraining

With an updated simulator and new live data, you can:

- Continue offline RL using logs from both shadow and live runs, exploiting off-policy algorithms designed for batch data.
- Perform periodic or continuous fine-tuning of the policy in the improved simulator, incorporating new regimes and stress events.
- Incorporate explicit regime-detection features (e.g., volatility and liquidity indicators) into the state, allowing the policy to adapt within a single model rather than via manual switching.

This creates a feedback loop: the simulator trains the policy, the policy's live performance reveals deficiencies in the simulator, which is then updated and used to train the next-generation policy.

In this section we moved from theoretical descriptions of the limit order book to the practical problem of simulating it for RL-based execution:

- We argued that microstructure detail—order types, matching rules, queue dynamics, impact, and latency—is essential for training realistic RL agents.
- We described how to construct LOB simulators using historical replay, parametric models, or generative approaches, and how to calibrate them to match stylized market facts.
- We introduced domain randomization and ensemble scenarios to improve robustness against simulator mis-specification.
- We advocated conservative RL objectives and explicit constraints to reduce the risk of brittle strategies.
- We outlined a staged deployment path from shadow mode to limited live rollout and full production, emphasizing continuous monitoring and slippage attribution.
- Finally, we emphasized the ongoing feedback loop between live experience, simulator refinement, and policy retraining.

Taken together, these elements form an integrated "execution RL stack" in which simulators and policies co-evolve with market microstructure, enabling data-driven execution strategies that are both powerful and operationally safe.

Chapter 6

Evaluation, Governance, and Production Deployment

Most reinforcement learning projects in finance fail not because the ideas are bad, but because the evaluation is sloppy and the production story is vague. In this chapter we move past toy results and paper Sharpe ratios to confront the real questions: How do you know your policy isn't overfit to a single bull market? What happens when the regime flips overnight? Who is accountable when an agent "learns" to game a benchmark or a regulatory rule? And how do you train at scale without breaking your latency budget on the exchange gateway? We will build a complete path from leakage-free backtests and walk-forward validation, through online experiments and model risk governance, to low-latency serving and attribution reports that portfolio managers and regulators can actually trust.

6.1 Backtesting Methodology and Temporal Cross-Validation

In the previous chapters we defined RL formulations for portfolio allocation and execution, and we described how to construct financial Markov decision processes (MDPs) and realistic market simulators. We now face the central practical question: *how do we evaluate an RL agent before putting real money at risk?*

A backtest is our best attempt to answer: "If this policy had been live in the past, what would have happened?" In reinforcement learning this question is more delicate than in supervised learning, because the policy takes a *sequence* of actions that interacts with the environment. Small modeling mistakes or data leaks can easily create the illusion of a profitable strategy.

This section develops a disciplined methodology for leakage-free backtesting in RL for finance, with three main goals:

- Ensure that the agent only sees information that would have been available at the decision time.
- Incorporate realistic trading frictions so that simulated performance is comparable to live trading.
- Use time-aware cross-validation schemes so that policy and hyperparameter choices are based on *genuinely* out-of-sample performance.

Typical Failure Modes of RL Backtests

Before constructing a robust methodology, it is useful to understand how things commonly go wrong. The mistakes below are easy to make, especially when re-using generic machine learning tooling that was not designed for time series.

Look-Ahead Bias in Features or Targets

Look-ahead bias occurs whenever you accidentally use future information to predict the past. In RL, this can affect:

- **State features.** Suppose you build a feature that uses the day's close price, but your policy makes decisions at 10:00. If you feed the closing price into the 10:00 state, the agent is implicitly given the future.
- **Returns and rewards.** When you construct episode rewards from future path information (for example, full-day implementation shortfall known at the end of the day) and then derive state features that depend on that full path, you may implicitly leak future realizations into earlier states.
- **Aggregated indicators.** Daily volatility estimates, rolling betas, or factor exposures that are calculated using both past and future observations (for example, centered rolling windows) introduce look-ahead if their future part is available to the agent.

For RL, look-ahead bias is especially dangerous because the agent can systematically exploit tiny predictive advantages. A small leak that would only mildly inflate a supervised learning model's accuracy can lead an RL agent to discover unrealistically profitable policies.

Label Leakage via Adjustments and Corporate Actions

Market data often includes "cleaned" prices and volumes:

- Prices are back-adjusted for splits and extraordinary dividends.
- Index constituents are provided as of today, not as of the historical date.
- Delisted securities may be removed entirely.

If you train an agent on such data without care, you implicitly reveal the future. For example, back-adjusted prices can change the apparent pre-split trajectory of a stock, causing the model to see smooth series that would not have been observable in real time. Similarly, if your universe at time t includes only stocks that *survive* until the present, you are excluding past losers and bankrupt entities, creating *survivorship bias*.

Survivorship Bias in Universe Selection

Survivorship bias arises when you condition on the asset still being present at the end of your sample. Two common forms are:

- **Equity universes.** Using today's index membership (for example, today's S&P 500 constituents) for all historical periods.
- **Broker symbols.** Using only instruments that are currently tradable on the platform, ignoring those that were delisted or merged.

An RL agent trained on such a "clean" universe will learn in an unrealistically benign environment, where extreme negative events and illiquid names are under-represented.

Reward Shaping with Future Path Information

Reinforcement learning often uses reward shaping to stabilize training or reflect business objectives. However, careless shaping can cause subtle data leaks. For instance:

- Adding a penalty based on the eventual maximum drawdown over an entire episode to each intermediate reward.
- Using the day's realized volume-weighted average price (VWAP) at the time of the first action.
- Distributing a full-day implementation shortfall back over intraday steps using information that would not have been known when those steps were taken.

The key principle is simple: *the reward at time t may depend on future prices in the simulator, but the* state *at time t must not.* The agent should only condition on what was observable when the decision was made.

Building a Realistic RL Trading Simulator

To backtest an RL agent, you need an environment that approximates how the real market would have responded to the agent's orders. This simulator is the bridge between historical data and hypothetical actions.

Granularity: Bar-Level vs. Order-Book Level

At the simplest level, one might simulate trading using bar data (for example, 1-minute OHLCV). The policy observes bar features and trades at the bar's close or mid-price, paying an assumed spread and transaction cost. This may be acceptable for higher-frequency portfolio rebalancing or for pedagogical examples.

For smart execution and routing, this is not enough. You need to model:

- **Bid-ask spread dynamics.** The spread is not constant; it widens in volatile periods and in illiquid names.
- **Order book depth.** Large market orders move the price; small ones may not.
- **Queue position and partial fills.** A limit order may not be fully filled; fill probability depends on queue position and subsequent order flow.

An order-book simulator replays historical limit order book snapshots or events, and injects the agent's orders into that stream, matching them against historical liquidity with a chosen impact model. Even if you cannot afford full tick-level replay, a layered approximation—for example, modeling the first few levels of the book plus a simple impact curve—is preferable to assuming frictionless execution.

Modeling Slippage, Costs, and Constraints

A key step toward realism is to incorporate trading frictions:

- **Explicit costs.** Broker commissions, exchange fees, and taxes (such as stamp duties or transaction taxes in some markets).
- **Implicit costs.** Bid-ask spread, price impact, and slippage relative to reference prices (mid, open, close, VWAP).
- **Constraints.** Position limits, inventory bounds, risk limits, and capital usage constraints.

For many use cases, a simple linear cost model is a reasonable starting point:

$$\text{cost} = \text{fixed\_fee} + c_{bps} \times |\text{notional}|,$$

where c_{bps} is the assumed cost in basis points of traded notional. You might augment this with a nonlinear impact term that increases with participation rate.

In the simulator, each executed order should:

- Determine a realistic execution price (for example, mid plus half-spread for market orders, or worse if size is large).
- Deduct explicit and implicit costs from the agent's cash or P&L.
- Update inventory and enforce constraints (for instance, blocking orders that would breach risk limits).

Calendars, Suspensions, and Events

Real markets are irregular. Trading halts, holidays, and corporate events break the smoothness that many machine learning pipelines implicitly assume. A realistic RL environment must:

- Respect **exchange calendars**: no trading on holidays or outside session hours; half-day schedules, auctions, and extended hours if relevant.

- Handle **suspensions and halts**: the agent should not be able to trade during a halt. The simulator can represent this by rejecting orders or by skipping time steps where no trades occur.
- Incorporate **corporate actions**: splits, dividends, rights issues, symbol changes. Price and volume data should be transformed in a way that preserves what was observable at each time, without retroactively modifying the past.

A practical approach is to maintain two layers of data:

- A "raw" layer reflecting prices and volumes as originally published.
- A "research" layer that is forward-consistent, with adjustments that do not leak future information (for example, adjusting past prices only using information that was known by that date, or using split factors that are applied from the split date onward rather than retroactively).

The environment should be built on the research layer, with explicit time indices and calendar logic so that every state and action is tied to a real-world timestamp.

Temporal Cross-Validation for RL Policies

Once we can simulate realistic trajectories, we need a systematic way to estimate how well a policy will perform on unseen data. Standard k-fold cross-validation, which randomly shuffles data into folds, is inappropriate for time series because it violates chronological ordering and encourages leakage.

Instead, we use *temporal* cross-validation schemes that preserve time order.

Rolling Window Evaluation

In a rolling window scheme, we:

- Choose a training window length (for example, three years of data).
- Choose a validation or test window length (for example, six months).
- Slide this pair forward through time.

Concretely:

- Window 1: Train on Years 1–3, validate on first half of Year 4.
- Window 2: Train on Years 1.5–3.5, validate on second half of Year 4.
- Window 3: Train on Years 2–4, validate on first half of Year 5.

At each step, the RL agent is trained from scratch (or warm-started from prior parameters, if that reflects your production process) using only data up to the start of the validation period. It is then evaluated on the validation period, which is strictly later in time.

Rolling windows are useful when the data-generating process is evolving and you want to keep the training set focused on recent history.

Expanding (Anchored) Window Evaluation

In an expanding or anchored window scheme, the training set grows over time while the validation window moves forward:

- Window 1: Train on Years 1–2, validate on first half of Year 3.
- Window 2: Train on Years 1–2.5, validate on second half of Year 3.
- Window 3: Train on Years 1–3, validate on first half of Year 4.

This approach mirrors a production process in which you continually append new data but retain the full historical archive. It is appropriate for strategies that are expected to benefit from long histories (for example, low-turnover portfolios or long-horizon macro strategies), while still respecting chronology.

Aligning with RL Training Horizon and Policy Refresh

RL training is computationally expensive, and policies often need to be refreshed periodically. Temporal cross-validation should be designed around the intended operational cadence:

- For a daily-rebalanced portfolio policy, you might retrain monthly or quarterly; your validation windows can be monthly blocks.
- For an intra-day execution agent, you might retrain on a rolling set of recent weeks, validating on the next few days.

In each window, you must decide:

- **How long an episode is.** Long episodes (for example, multi-day) may require careful alignment with validation intervals so that entire episodes fall within the training or validation set, not split across.
- **How much exploration is allowed.** In a pure backtest, you replay historical data; the agent cannot actually explore new actions that would have changed the past. Your training algorithm must be off-policy, or your simulator must model how actions would have altered the environment, as discussed in earlier chapters.

The key rule is that *no information from the validation period may influence the training process in that window.* This includes tuning hyperparameters, selecting network architectures, or choosing reward shaping schemes. All of those choices must be based only on past windows or a dedicated development set.

Nested Cross-Validation for Hyperparameter and Model Selection

Model selection itself can become a source of overfitting if you repeatedly examine validation performance and tweak the design until you "find" a profitable policy. To mitigate this, we can use *nested* temporal cross-validation:

- An **inner loop** over multiple training/validation splits, used to choose hyperparameters and other design decisions.
- An **outer loop** that holds out one or more evaluation periods that are *never* used during design or tuning.

For example:

- Use Years 1–6 in several rolling windows (Years 1–4 train, 4–5 validate; 1.5–4.5 train, 4.5–5.5 validate; etc.) to tune hyperparameters and architecture.
- Once design is fixed, retrain using Years 1–6 and evaluate once on Years 6–7 as an *outer test set.*

This outer test performance is your best estimate of how the policy may behave on truly unseen data. It should be reported once, at the end of the research cycle, and not reused for further tuning.

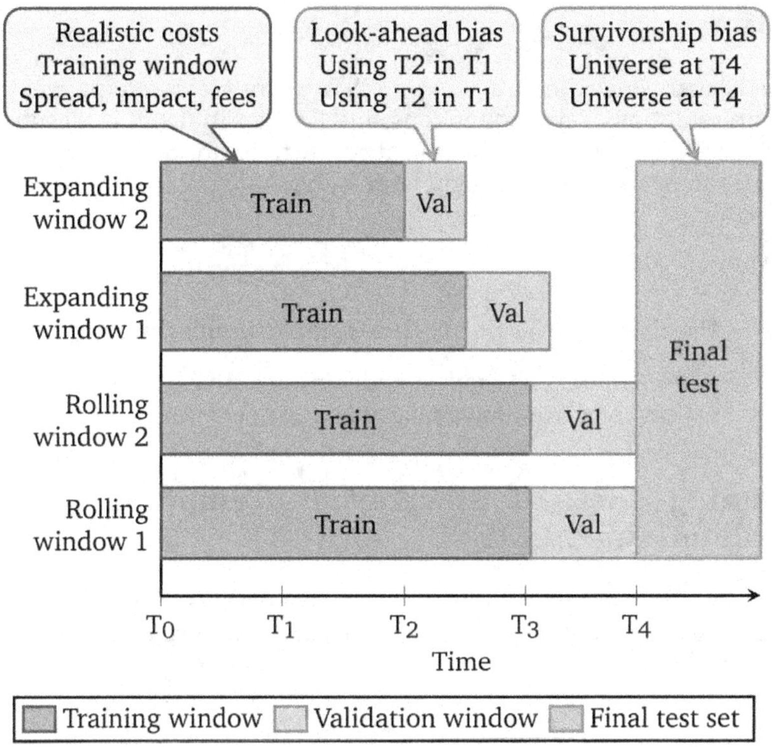

Splitting Data Across Research, Tuning, and Final Evaluation

To put the above ideas into practice, it is useful to think of the full historical sample as being partitioned into three conceptual blocks:

- A **research set** for exploration and prototyping.
- A **tuning set** for systematic temporal cross-validation and model selection.
- A **final test set** for one-time evaluation of the chosen approach.

Research Set: Exploration and Hypothesis Generation

In the early stages of a project, you will try many ideas: alternative state representations, reward functions, and RL algorithms. It is acceptable to use a portion of the historical data quite freely for this purpose, with the understanding that insights drawn here are informal and may be biased.

Typical guidelines:

- Use the earliest segment of the sample for this research set.
- Expect to discard models and results derived here; they serve mainly to narrow down plausible design choices.

Tuning Set: Structured Temporal Cross-Validation

Once you have a small number of candidate designs, reserve a contiguous time block that follows the research set as your tuning set. Within this period, implement rolling or expanding temporal cross-validation:

- Define several windows that mimic your planned retraining cadence.
- For each candidate design, train and evaluate across all windows.
- Compare performance using metrics aligned with your business objective (for example, risk-adjusted return, implementation shortfall, or cost savings).

The tuning set is where you commit to a systematic model selection process. You should document:

- Which windows were used.
- Which metrics drove decisions.
- How many candidate designs were compared.

This documentation will be valuable for internal review and later governance.

Final Test Set: One-Shot Performance Estimation

The final test set is the last contiguous block of history, held back from any design or tuning work. Its purpose is to provide an honest, unbiased estimate of live performance.

- Train your chosen design using the same procedure you intend for production, on all data up to the start of the test set.
- Evaluate exactly once on the test set, using the same simulator, cost model, and reporting metrics that will be used for live monitoring.
- Resist the temptation to tweak the design based on test results. If you do, you must treat that test as contaminated and either accept a biased estimate or allocate a new, later test period.

For long-horizon strategies, the test set may need to span several years to include enough independent episodes and market regimes. For intra-day execution agents, a shorter but more granular period may suffice, as long as it contains diverse volatility and liquidity states.

Putting It All Together: Practical Guidelines

We conclude with a set of practical guidelines that synthesize this section into a workflow you can implement.

- **Freeze the data and universe.** Start by defining a historical dataset with a fixed universe for each date, including delisted and illiquid names. Generate a forward-consistent research layer that avoids look-ahead from corporate actions.
- **Define state and reward pipelines with strict time indexing.** Explicitly tag each feature with the timestamp at which it becomes available. Build the environment so that the state at time t only includes features whose availability time is $\leq t$.

- **Choose a cost model and constraints that reflect intended trading size and venues.** Calibrate costs using historical trades or broker schedules where possible. Implement these costs in the simulator so that every action the agent takes incurs a realistic penalty.
- **Design episodes to match operational reality.** For portfolio problems, an episode might span months or quarters; for execution, it might be a single order or basket. Align episode boundaries with your temporal cross-validation windows.
- **Implement rolling or expanding temporal cross-validation on the tuning set.** Decide on window lengths, overlaps, and retraining cadences that reflect how you will maintain the policy in production.
- **Use nested cross-validation for model selection when feasible.** Avoid overfitting to a single validation period by evaluating candidate designs across multiple windows before choosing a final approach.
- **Reserve a final test period and treat it as sacrosanct.** Use it only once, after all design decisions are frozen. Report its results transparently, including any limitations or unusual market conditions it contains.
- **Document assumptions and limitations.** For every backtest, record the key modeling choices: universe, data sources, simulator approximations, cost model, constraints, cross-validation scheme, and any known biases. This documentation feeds directly into the governance and model risk management frameworks discussed in later sections.

A leakage-free, friction-aware, and time-respecting backtest does not guarantee success in live trading—markets will continue to change, and simulators are never perfect. However, it is a necessary foundation. Without it, reinforcement learning agents will happily exploit artifacts of your data pipeline instead of structure in the market, leading to fragile policies that fail on first contact with reality. In the next section, we build on this foundation to examine how such agents should be evaluated and governed once they begin operating in live or paper markets.

6.2 Online Experiments, Model Risk, and Drift Monitoring

In the previous section we focused on offline evaluation: carefully constructed backtests and temporal cross-validation schemes that mimic future deployment while avoiding data leakage. Offline work is necessary, but it is not sufficient. Markets are nonstationary, simulators are approximate, and reinforcement learning (RL) agents can behave in surprising ways once they interact with live order flow.

This section explains how to move from offline evidence to live experimentation in a way that is controlled, observable, and reversible. We will:

- Introduce online evaluation patterns such as shadow trading and canary rollouts.
- Frame RL trading systems from a model risk perspective, highlighting failure modes that backtests may miss.
- Describe monitoring tools that detect regime shifts and policy drift.
- Define kill-switches and safe fallback behaviors that bound damage when things go wrong.

The overarching goal is to treat live deployment as an ongoing experiment rather than a one-time "launch," and to ensure that every experiment has clear guardrails.

From Offline Confidence to Online Caution

A strong backtest and temporal cross-validation tell you that a policy would have worked *if* the future resembled the past and your simulator were perfect. In practice:

- Market regimes change: volatility, liquidity, and crowding vary over time.

- Microstructure changes: tick sizes, fee schedules, and venue behaviors evolve.
- Your own model may change markets: a new source of flow can move prices or alter queue dynamics.

Consequently, the first time a policy interacts with live markets should be treated as the beginning of a new learning phase. The experiments you run in production are as important as the experiments you ran in backtesting.

Two principles guide this phase:

- **Progressive exposure.** Start with zero or tiny risk, observe behavior, and only then scale up.
- **Continuous diagnosis.** Instrument the policy so you can detect unexpected behavior and regime shifts promptly.

Online Evaluation Patterns

We begin with deployment patterns that let you collect information about a new RL policy while limiting downside.

Shadow Trading

In shadow trading, the RL agent runs in parallel to the existing production strategy, but its actions are not actually sent to the market. Instead:

- The live market data feed is mirrored to the RL policy.
- At each decision time, the agent proposes an action (for example, new portfolio weights or order slices).
- The proposed action is logged along with the current state, but the *legacy* or *baseline* strategy continues to control trading.

Using the logged proposals and realized market prices, you can simulate what would have happened if the RL agent had been in control. This has several benefits:

- You obtain a genuinely out-of-sample and out-of-backtest performance estimate.
- You see how the policy behaves under real data glitches, latency spikes, and other operational issues.
- You can compare the RL policy's decisions with the baseline in real time, looking for obviously unreasonable actions.

Shadow trading is especially attractive for complex RL agents or for strategies with high model risk, because it exposes the agent to live conditions without any capital at risk.

Canary or Pilot Rollouts

Once shadow trading looks promising, the next step is often a *canary* or *pilot* rollout. The name comes from the "canary in the coal mine" metaphor: a small, sacrificial system that reveals problems before they become severe.

In a canary rollout:

- A small fraction of capital or order flow is routed through the RL policy.
- The remainder continues to be handled by the baseline strategy.
- Tight risk limits and monitoring rules apply specifically to the canary.

For example, an execution agent might be allowed to handle at most 5% of daily volume for a subset of liquid instruments, with hard caps on intraday loss and slippage versus a benchmark. If any of these caps are breached, the canary is automatically disabled and all flow reverts to the baseline.

Canary deployments give you two crucial pieces of information:

- How the RL agent interacts with its own impact on the market, which shadow trading cannot fully capture.
- How the operational stack behaves end-to-end: from signal generation to order routing, backtesting cost models, and risk checks.

A/B and Multivariate Experiments

When both the RL policy and the baseline are live on some fraction of flow, you can design controlled experiments similar in spirit to A/B tests on websites, but with important differences:

- **Delayed outcomes.** For portfolios, the outcome of a decision may only be observable days or weeks later.
- **Autocorrelation.** Returns and order flows are autocorrelated; observations are not independent.
- **Interference.** The presence of both policies can influence market conditions or each other (for example, if both trade the same instruments).

To handle these issues:

- Randomize at the right level: for execution, randomize at the order or basket level (policy A vs. policy B); for portfolios, randomize across client accounts or internal sub-portfolios when allowed.
- Define metrics that account for autocorrelation: compare average implementation shortfall, risk-adjusted P&L, or cost savings over many days, not trade-by-trade.
- Use block randomization: assign policies in contiguous time blocks (for example, alternating days or weeks) so that both experience similar conditions over the experiment horizon.

For complex desks, you may run multivariate experiments where several policy variants share flow. In that case, keep the number of variants small relative to the signal in the metrics; otherwise you risk underpowered experiments and noisy conclusions.

Model Risk in RL Trading Systems

Any predictive model carries risk, but RL agents add additional dimensions:

- They optimize long-horizon objectives that may be mis-specified.
- They rely on an environment model (the simulator) that is inevitably approximate.
- They may be re-trained periodically, introducing instability.
- Their behavior can be hard to predict from static tests because it emerges from sequential decisions.

A model risk perspective asks: *what could go wrong, even if the implementation is correct?*

Sources of Model Risk

Key sources of model risk for RL in finance include:

Reward Misspecification.

The reward function may not perfectly encode the business objective or constraints. Examples:

- An execution agent rewarded solely on implementation shortfall might learn to systematically underfill difficult orders to appear cheap, shifting risk back to the portfolio manager.
- A market-making agent rewarded on spread capture but not sufficiently penalized for inventory risk might accumulate large, one-sided positions in illiquid markets.

Environment Misspecification.

The simulator used during training may differ materially from the live market:

- Order book dynamics that ignore other large participants or venue-specific matching rules.
- Cost models calibrated on outdated fee schedules or spread regimes.

The policy may exploit quirks of the simulator that do not generalize.

Data and Regime Drift.

Input distributions change over time:

- Volatility and correlations shift across regimes.
- New instruments or venues are introduced; others become obsolete.
- Market microstructure evolves with regulation and technology.

The RL policy, trained on past data, may no longer be appropriate for the new environment.

Policy Instability Under Retraining.

Because RL training is noisy and non-convex, small changes in hyperparameters or data can lead to large changes in behavior. Even if average performance is similar, path-wise differences can be uncomfortable for risk managers and clients.

Emergent Pathologies.

RL agents can learn to "game" benchmarks or exploit loopholes:

- Concentrating risk in rare states that are under-weighted in the reward.
- Exploiting unintended correlations in features that are fragile.
- Oscillating or churning inventory in ways that pass risk checks but increase hidden costs.

Online experiments and monitoring must be designed to surface these risks early.

Regime Detection and Drift Monitoring

Once a policy handles real flow, you need to track how both the *environment* and the *policy* evolve through time. Monitoring should not be an afterthought; it is a core part of the RL system.

Environment and Regime Indicators

The first set of monitors focuses on the market environment:

- **Volatility state.** Rolling estimates of realized volatility at relevant horizons (intra-day for execution, daily or longer for portfolios) to detect calm vs. stressed regimes.
- **Liquidity state.** Effective spreads, top-of-book depth, and realized market impact per unit of traded volume.
- **Factor exposures.** For portfolio RL, rolling regressions of portfolio returns on risk factors (for example, value, momentum, size) to see whether the strategy's risk profile is drifting.

These indicators help you answer: *is the market similar to the conditions on which the policy was trained and validated?* When the answer is "no," performance deviations become easier to interpret.

Reward and P&L Distribution Shifts

The next layer looks at outcomes:

- Distributions of daily or intra-day P&L relative to backtest expectations.
- Implementation shortfall, VWAP/TWAP slippage, and other execution metrics for execution agents.
- Drawdowns and tail losses relative to historical simulations.

You can compare these distributions over rolling windows to those from the backtest or from an earlier live period. Large, sustained deviations may indicate that the reward function is misaligned with actual business objectives in the current regime or that the environment has shifted.

Action-Distribution and Policy Diagnostics

Finally, you want to monitor the *decisions* themselves, not just their outcomes. Relevant signals include:

- **Action distribution drift.** Changes in the frequency of key actions: for example, the proportion of time the agent chooses aggressive vs. passive orders, or large vs. small size adjustments.

- **State-conditional behavior.** How actions change as a function of volatility, liquidity, time-of-day, or inventory levels. For instance, does the agent still de-risk in high volatility, as it did in backtests?
- **Policy-value diagnostics.** For value-based methods, tracking the predicted value function vs. realized returns; large systematic biases may indicate off-policy shift or value overestimation.

A simple but powerful tool is to compute divergences (such as Kullback-Leibler divergence) between action distributions in the backtest and in live trading, stratified by key state variables. Large divergences signal that the agent is behaving in qualitatively new ways and merits closer inspection.

Kill-Switches and Safe Fallback Behaviors

Monitoring is useful only if it feeds into actions. In trading, you need clearly defined mechanisms that can override or disable the RL policy when necessary.

Hard and Soft Kill-Switches

Soft kill-switches are automated de-risking actions that respond to elevated but not catastrophic signals. Examples:

- Temporarily reducing the fraction of flow allocated to the RL policy.
- Tightening inventory or risk limits.
- Switching the agent into a “defensive” mode (for example, using more passive orders, widening participation bands).

Hard kill-switches fully disable the RL agent for some or all instruments:

- Routing all orders back to a static baseline or rule-based strategy.
- Freezing policy updates and exploration.

- Requiring manual approval for any further deployment.

Triggers for hard kill-switches should be quantitative, documented in advance, and visible to both the trading desk and risk management. Typical triggers include:

- Breach of pre-defined loss or drawdown limits over specified horizons.
- Slippage or execution quality metrics exceeding thresholds relative to the baseline.
- Detected technical failures, such as loss of connectivity to market data or risk engines.

Safe Baseline Policies

A kill-switch is only useful if there is something safe to fall back on. Safe baselines are usually:

- **Simple.** For example, static allocation rules, TWAP/VWAP schedules, or conservative participation bands that have been used historically.
- **Transparent.** Their behavior is well understood by traders and risk managers.
- **Operationally robust.** Implemented on stable infrastructure with a strong track record.

During canary and A/B phases, the baseline runs continuously in parallel, which naturally supports instant fallback: turning off the RL path simply routes all flow through the baseline.

An Integrated Online Deployment Loop

Putting the pieces together, we can view online experimentation and monitoring as a closed loop:

- A candidate RL policy is selected based on offline evaluation.

- The policy is deployed in shadow trading, collecting behavior and counterfactual performance.
- If results are favorable, the policy moves to canary rollout with small flow, under strict monitoring.
- Drift and performance signals are continuously monitored at environment, outcome, and policy levels.
- If metrics remain within agreed limits, exposure may be gradually increased; if not, soft or hard kill-switches revert to the safe baseline.
- Insights from online experiments feed back into model design, simulator calibration, and risk limits.

The following diagram illustrates this loop.

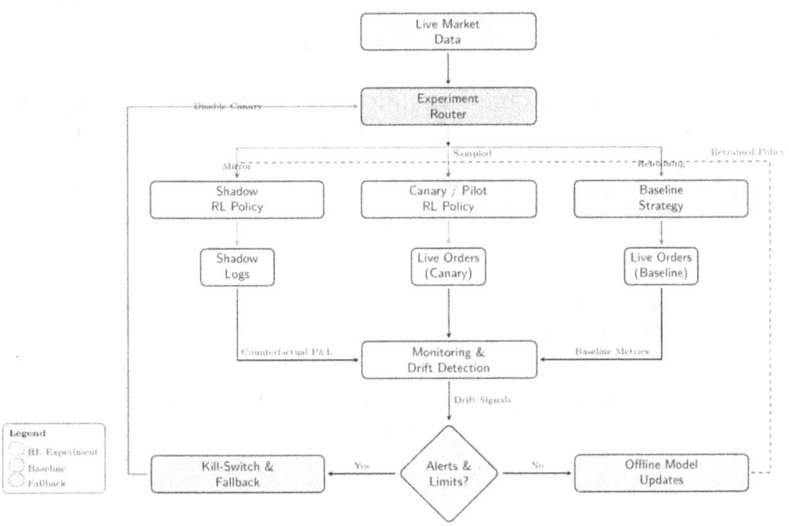

Summary and Outlook

This section has extended the evaluation lens from offline backtests to live, controlled experimentation. We have seen that:

- Shadow trading and canary rollouts allow RL policies to be tested under real conditions with bounded risk.
- RL-specific model risks—reward misspecification, environment mismatch, retraining instability, and emergent pathologies—require dedicated attention.
- Drift monitoring must cover the environment, outcomes, and policy behavior, and must be wired into clear soft and hard kill-switches with safe baselines.
- Online deployment is not a once-and-for-all event but a continuous loop of experimentation, monitoring, and refinement.

In the next section we will connect these practices to the broader regulatory and governance context, showing how best-execution obligations, market integrity, and auditability shape how RL strategies are approved, reviewed, and overseen.

6.3 Regulatory Compliance and Best-Execution Governance

The previous sections have focused on *how well* an RL trading system performs: first offline, through leakage-free backtests, and then online, via controlled experiments and drift monitoring. In a real institution, however, performance is only one dimension. Trading systems live inside a regulatory and organizational environment that places obligations around *how* orders are executed, *how* risks are controlled, and *how* decisions are documented and overseen.

This section explains how RL-based trading and execution systems fit into that environment. We will:

- Map regulatory themes such as best execution, market integrity, suitability, and record-keeping onto RL agents.
- Show how to express an RL agent's mandate and constraints in clear policy language.

- Describe controls and audit trails that make RL systems explainable, reviewable, and accountable.
- Outline a governance lifecycle for RL models, from approval through change-management to decommissioning.

The central message is that reinforcement learning does not replace governance; it makes governance more important. Powerful, adaptive systems must be anchored in a strong framework of accountability.

Regulatory Themes in the RL Context

Regulatory details differ across jurisdictions, but the high-level themes are remarkably consistent. RL systems engage with at least four of them.

Best Execution

Best execution obligations require an investment firm to take *all reasonable steps* to obtain the best possible result for clients, considering price, costs, speed, likelihood of execution, and other factors. For RL systems this means:

- The *objective* the agent is trained on should correspond to a defensible interpretation of best execution for the relevant products and clients.
- The firm must be able to explain, in words, how the agent typically balances price improvement, fill probability, and market impact.
- Post-trade analysis must compare actual outcomes to benchmarks (for example, arrival price, VWAP) and to alternative routes (for example, internal baseline algorithms).

If the RL agent systematically chooses actions that save explicit fees but increase implicit market impact, for instance, the firm may be challenged on whether it is truly achieving best execution.

Market Integrity and Market Abuse

Supervisors are concerned that automated trading systems, if left unchecked, may:

- Disrupt fair and orderly markets (for example, through runaway feedback loops or excessive quote traffic).
- Engage in abusive behaviors such as spoofing, layering, or other forms of deceptive order placement.

An RL agent trained purely on short-term P&L could—at least in principle—discover strategies that exploit microstructure in ways that are inconsistent with market integrity, especially if the simulator fails to encode prohibitions on abusive patterns. The governance framework must therefore ensure that:

- Certain behaviors are explicitly forbidden in the action space or constrained via pre-trade checks.
- Post-trade surveillance can detect patterns associated with market abuse, even if generated autonomously by an agent.
- The firm retains the ability, and the obligation, to intervene when behavior appears suspicious, regardless of whether it arises from human or algorithmic decisions.

Suitability and Client Mandates

At the portfolio level, suitability rules require that trading strategies be appropriate for the client's objectives, risk tolerance, and investment horizon. In an RL setting this implies:

- Each RL policy must be attached to a clear mandate describing which accounts or products it may manage.
- The reward function and constraints for that policy must align with the mandate. A high-turnover, leverage-seeking RL strategy is not suitable for a low-risk income fund.
- Changes to the policy that materially affect risk or behavior should be reviewed for suitability, not just technical performance.

Record-Keeping and Auditability

Regulators expect firms to retain detailed records of orders, executions, and the rationale behind them. For traditional strategies, that rationale might be a trader's notes or an investment committee's minutes. For RL systems, the rationale is encoded in data, model parameters, and policy logic. Governance must therefore ensure:

- Sufficient data is stored to reconstruct what the agent *saw* and *decided* at each point.
- Model versions and configuration states are captured and linked to trades.
- The firm can later explain, to regulators and clients, why a given pattern of behavior occurred.

Defining the RL Agent's Mandate and Constraints

Before training or deploying an RL system, you should be able to describe its intended role in simple, non-technical language. This is the *mandate*. Around this mandate you then wrap quantitative constraints that bound behavior.

Plain-Language Mandates

A mandate statement might look like:

> "This RL policy provides intra-day execution of equity orders for large-cap stocks in market X, with the objective of minimizing implementation shortfall relative to arrival price, while respecting client-specific urgency and risk constraints."

or

> "This RL policy manages the currency hedge for global equity portfolios, targeting a 50% hedge ratio with tolerance bands, and seeking to minimize transaction costs subject to tracking the benchmark hedge over a monthly horizon."

Such descriptions are valuable for several reasons:

- They allow non-technical stakeholders—traders, risk managers, compliance—to understand what the agent is allowed to do.
- They force the quant team to connect the RL formulation (state, action, reward) to business concepts (urgency, hedge ratio, benchmark).
- They serve as a reference point for later questions about scope creep or use in unintended contexts.

Codifying Risk Constraints and Forbidden Behaviors

The next layer is to translate risk and compliance requirements into explicit constraints. These may include:

- **Position and inventory limits:** maximum gross and net exposure, concentration caps by instrument, sector, or currency.
- **Order and message throttles:** maximum order rate, quote-to-trade ratios, and notional per order, to protect market integrity and infrastructure.
- **Venue and instrument restrictions:** blacklists of venues or products; constraints around dark pools or internalization depending on best-execution policies.
- **Leverage and liquidity rules:** minimum liquidity thresholds for tradable instruments; leverage caps at portfolio level.

In RL terms, you can apply these constraints in several ways:

- *Action-space design:* exclude actions that violate constraints, so the policy never proposes them.
- *Pre-trade risk checks:* evaluate each proposed action against constraint logic; block or modify actions that would breach limits.
- *Reward shaping:* penalize the agent for approaching soft limits or for using scarce risk capacity inefficiently.

Crucially, forbidden behaviors—such as patterns associated with spoofing—should be ruled out at the level of the trading system, not left for the agent to "learn" as suboptimal. Governance should treat them as non-negotiable constraints, similar to legal prohibitions on insider trading.

Pre-Trade and Post-Trade Controls

Controls are mechanisms that ensure the RL agent respects its mandate and constraints in real time, and that its performance can be evaluated after the fact.

Pre-Trade Controls

Pre-trade controls act as a protective filter between the agent and the market. Typical components include:

- **Limit checks:** verifying that a proposed order does not exceed size, price, or notional limits for the instrument and client.
- **Exposure checks:** ensuring that the resulting positions remain within portfolio risk limits across multiple dimensions (for example, sector, factor, currency).
- **Market condition checks:** blocking or transforming actions during certain conditions (for example, auctions, halts, severe volatility spikes) where the agent was not trained or where behavior is more tightly controlled.
- **Behavioral rules:** rejecting order patterns (for example, rapid cancel-replace sequences at the top of the book) that could be misinterpreted as abusive, even if the agent finds them profitable.

In implementation, these controls should be applied uniformly regardless of whether the order was initiated by an RL agent or by a human trader. This both simplifies the system and reinforces the notion that RL is just another way of generating trading instructions within the same governance perimeter.

Post-Trade Controls and Surveillance

After trades are executed, post-trade systems check that behavior was consistent with best execution, mandates, and market integrity. For RL systems this involves:

- **Execution quality analysis:** comparing realized execution prices to benchmarks (arrival, VWAP, midpoint) and to the performance of baseline algorithms or external brokers.
- **Pattern surveillance:** scanning for suspicious patterns such as layering, quote stuffing, or wash trades, using established compliance tools but applied to RL-generated flow.
- **Mandate adherence checks:** verifying that portfolios stayed within stated risk profiles, hedge ratios, and other mandate-specific boundaries.

Importantly, these analyses should be able to distinguish between the RL policy and other sources of flow, so that any issues can be traced back to the correct system and addressed accordingly.

Audit Trails and Explainability

An RL trading system may involve deep networks, large state spaces, and complex dynamics. Regulators and internal committees are unlikely to accept "the neural network decided so" as a sufficient explanation. Instead, you need two complementary things:

- Rich, immutable *audit trails* that record the facts.
- *Explanation artifacts* that translate those facts into human-understandable narratives and metrics.

What to Log: Building an Audit Trail

At a minimum, for each action taken (and, ideally, for each action *considered*) by the RL system, you should log:

- A timestamp and unique identifier linking this decision to subsequent orders and executions.

- The **state features** supplied to the policy (or, if logging all features is impractical, a compressed summary and a way to reconstruct the features later from stored market data).
- The **policy identifier**: model version, training dataset range, hyperparameter configuration, and any relevant settings.
- The **recommended action** (for example, target weights, order type and size, venue choice) and any **overrides** or modifications made by pre-trade checks or human intervention.
- The **realized outcome**: fills, prices, costs, and subsequent P&L attribution associated with this decision.

These logs should be tamper-evident and stored in a way that satisfies record-keeping requirements for the relevant business (often several years). They provide the raw material for both day-to-day monitoring and post-incident investigations.

Making Behavior Explainable

On top of raw logs, you need higher-level tools to articulate how and why the RL policy behaves as it does. Examples include:

- **Policy summaries:** aggregated descriptions such as "the agent tends to trade more aggressively when spread is narrow and order book depth is high," backed by conditional statistics.
- **Scenario-based analysis:** replaying specific historical episodes (for example, a volatility spike) and comparing the RL policy's actions and P&L to those of the baseline or a simple heuristic.
- **Attribution reports:** decomposing returns or execution quality into contributions from different decision levers (venue choice, order type, timing), as discussed later in the chapter.
- **Sensitivity checks:** stress tests showing how the policy's decisions change when certain inputs are perturbed (for example, slightly higher volatility, thinner liquidity), to demonstrate robustness.

Explainability does not necessarily mean opening up the internal weights of the network to inspection. In practice, regulators and senior management are more interested in whether the system's *observable behavior* is understandable, aligned with stated objectives, and stable under plausible changes in conditions.

Governance Lifecycle for RL Strategies

Finally, we embed RL strategies into a structured lifecycle of approval, monitoring, and change-management. This lifecycle should integrate quants, trading desks, risk, and compliance.

Model Approval

Before an RL strategy handles real client orders or firm capital, it should go through a formal approval process, typically involving a model or algorithmic trading committee. The approval package usually contains:

- A clear description of the mandate, objectives, and constraints.
- Offline evidence: backtests, temporal cross-validation, and sensitivity analyses.
- Online evidence: results from shadow trading and canary experiments, including performance vs. baseline and any observed pathologies.
- Risk assessments: identification of model risks (reward misspecification, environment mismatch, data drift), proposed monitoring indicators, and kill-switch triggers.
- Implementation details: system architecture, pre- and post-trade controls, logging, and fallback mechanisms.

Approval is not merely a sign-off on past performance—it is an endorsement of the full process by which the model will be monitored and updated.

Ongoing Monitoring and Periodic Review

Once live, the RL strategy should be subject to ongoing monitoring (as described in the previous section) and to periodic, higher-level reviews, for example quarterly or annually. These reviews might cover:

- Cumulative performance and risk relative to expectations and benchmarks.
- Evidence of regime shifts or drift and how the strategy has responded.
- Incidents: times when kill-switches were triggered, overrides were frequent, or behavior raised concerns.
- Planned changes: retraining schedules, feature updates, or reward adjustments.

A periodic review provides an opportunity to re-evaluate whether the strategy is still fit for purpose, given evolving markets, regulations, and business needs.

Change-Management for Retraining and Feature Updates

Unlike many traditional models, RL policies are often re-trained on a schedule or in response to new data. Each retraining or significant change (for example, adding a new feature set, changing the action space, or modifying the reward) should follow a change-management process:

- **Impact assessment:** what aspects of behavior are expected to change, and why?
- **Testing plan:** which offline and online tests will be run (for example, backtest on new data, shadow trading, limited canary rollout)?
- **Approval thresholds:** what metrics must be satisfied relative to the current live version to justify promotion?
- **Rollback plan:** how quickly and under what conditions can the change be reversed?

It is helpful to treat each new trained policy as a versioned artifact in a model registry, with clear lineage to training data, code version, and previous models. Promotions from one version to the next should be traceable and auditable.

Incident Handling and Postmortems

Even with strong governance, incidents will occur: unexpected losses, technical failures, or behavior that appears inconsistent with mandates or best execution. A mature RL governance framework includes:

- Pre-defined escalation paths: who must be informed, and how quickly?
- Immediate containment steps: activating kill-switches, halting retraining, or restricting scope.
- Structured postmortems: reconstructing what happened using audit trails; identifying root causes in data, environment assumptions, reward design, or controls; and specifying remediation steps.

The purpose of postmortems is not to assign blame to a model or a person, but to strengthen the overall system: improving simulators, tightening constraints, refining monitoring, or adjusting the governance process itself.

RL-based trading and execution systems promise adaptive, high-performance decision-making, but they do so within a dense web of fiduciary duties and regulatory expectations. By:

- grounding RL mandates in plain language;
- embedding hard constraints and controls that enforce best execution and market integrity;
- building rich audit trails and explanation tools; and
- placing RL models inside a robust lifecycle of approval, monitoring, change-management, and postmortems,

firms can harness RL's potential while maintaining the accountability and transparency that regulators, clients, and internal stakeholders rightly demand.

In the next section we move from governance and policy back to engineering, describing the system architectures and infrastructure required to train RL agents at scale and serve them reliably in low-latency production environments.

6.4 System Architecture, Training at Scale, and Low-Latency Serving

The previous sections have treated RL trading systems as abstract policies evaluated in backtests and governed by procedures and controls. To make these policies operational, however, we need concrete systems: data pipelines, simulators, training clusters, and low-latency services that talk to exchanges and brokers.

This section steps back and looks at the end-to-end architecture that supports RL in production. We will:

- Separate the RL stack into *data*, *training*, and *serving* planes, each with its own responsibilities.
- Explain how to scale training using distributed experience collection and realistic simulators.
- Describe model registry and deployment workflows that connect research, governance, and production.
- Discuss design patterns for ultra-low-latency inference and robust serving.

Throughout, we focus on principles that apply broadly; the exact technologies will differ by firm.

Separating Data, Training, and Serving Planes

A common anti-pattern in early prototypes is a monolithic script or notebook that pulls data, trains a model, and then simulates orders, all in one place. This may suffice for research, but it is brittle and ungovernable in production.

A more robust design splits the RL system into three planes:

- The **data plane**, which ingests, cleans, and serves market and reference data, and generates features and replayable environments.
- The **training plane**, which runs RL algorithms over simulators or historical replays, coordinating actors and learners at scale.
- The **serving plane**, which exposes trained policies to live trading flows with strict latency and reliability objectives.

This separation has several advantages:

- It allows each plane to scale and evolve independently (for example, upgrading training hardware without touching live trading systems).
- It clarifies responsibilities across teams (data engineering, quant research, production engineering).
- It simplifies governance: changing a policy or feature can be reasoned about and tested within a given plane before it touches the others.

High-Level Architecture

Figure illustrates a high-level architecture that follows this separation.

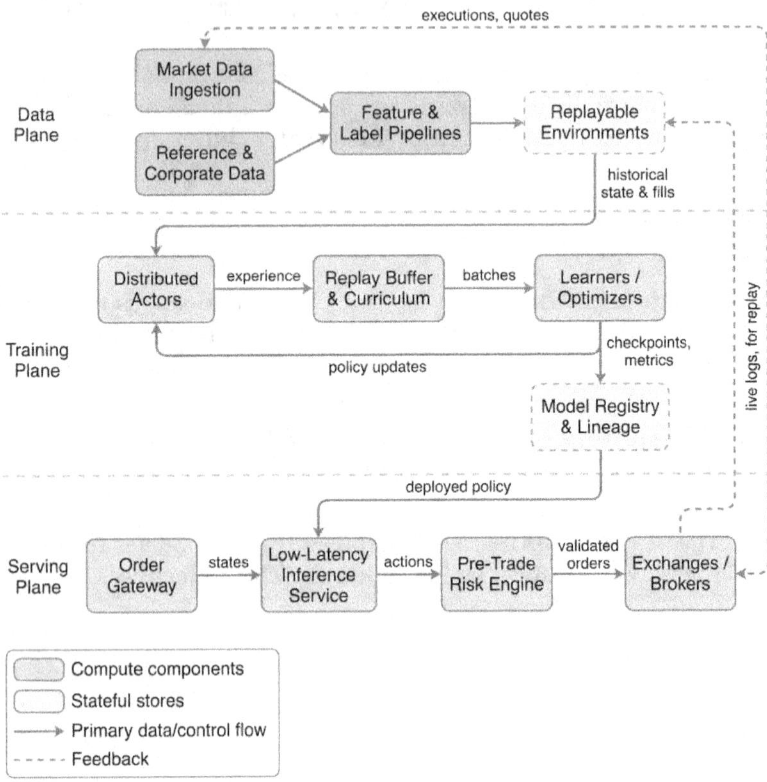

In the rest of the section we unpack each plane and the connections between them.

Data Plane: From Raw Feeds to Replayable Environments

The data plane supports both research and production. It provides:

- High-quality historical data for simulators and backtests.
- Live market data and reference updates for inference.

- Consistent feature definitions across training and serving.

Market and Reference Data Ingestion

At the base are market data feeds:

- **Trades and quotes:** tick-level data for order-book reconstruction, or bar data for lower-frequency strategies.
- **Reference data:** instrument metadata, corporate actions, index membership, trading calendars.
- **Derived indicators:** factor returns, benchmarks, risk-free curves.

These feeds are normalized and stored in a time-series database or data lake with clear versioning and timestamping. The same ingestion logic should produce both:

- Near-real-time views for the serving plane (with low lag but possibly incomplete corrections), and
- Backfilled, fully reconciled views for the research and training planes.

Feature and Label Pipelines

On top of raw data, feature pipelines construct the state representations used by the RL agents:

- Price and volume features (returns, volatility estimates, liquidity measures).
- Portfolio or order state (inventory, risk exposures, urgency).
- Market context (time-of-day, corporate event flags, volatility regimes).

A crucial design goal is *feature parity* between training and serving:

- The same transformation code, with the same parameters and lags, should run in both environments.
- Feature computation should respect availability times to avoid look-ahead, as discussed in earlier sections.

Label pipelines (in supervised learning) compute targets; in RL, they are more often used to:

- Provide auxiliary training signals (for example, factor returns).
- Compute performance metrics and rewards in simulators.

Replayable Environments

To train RL agents, we need environments that can replay historical market behavior while injecting hypothetical orders and state transitions. The environment layer:

- Reads from normalized market and reference data.
- Exposes a step interface: given an action at time t, returns the next state and reward, modeling fills, slippage, and constraints.
- Can be instantiated many times in parallel for distributed training.

Replayable environments also serve as a bridge between live trading and training: logs from production (states, actions, fills) can be fed back into the environment store, enabling off-policy evaluation, debugging, and future training.

Training Plane: Distributed RL at Scale

The training plane implements RL algorithms over the environments provided by the data plane. In finance, sample efficiency and training speed matter: you may need to explore large policy spaces and retrain frequently as data accumulates.

Actor-Learner Architectures

A common pattern for scalable RL is the actor-learner architecture:

- **Actors** run environment instances, executing the current policy to generate trajectories (states, actions, rewards).
- **Learners** consume experience from actors, compute gradients, and update policy parameters.
- A **parameter server** or synchronization protocol distributes updated parameters back to actors.

This allows:

- Linear scaling of experience collection by adding more actors.
- Separation of concerns: actors are I/O-bound on environment simulation; learners are compute-bound on optimization.

Depending on the algorithm (off-policy vs. on-policy) and the environment (pure historical replay vs. stylized simulator), you might choose:

- Synchronous updates (actors wait for learners each iteration) for more stable training.
- Asynchronous updates (actors continue while learners update in the background) for higher throughput at the cost of more "stale" policies on actors.

Replay Buffers and Curriculum Scheduling

For off-policy methods and complex environments, a replay buffer stores experience tuples (s, a, r, s') for reuse. In finance, replay design often includes:

- **Temporal structure:** preserving episode boundaries (for example, one execution order or one trading day) to allow sequence-based algorithms.

- **Prioritization:** emphasizing rare but informative events, such as large moves or illiquid conditions, via prioritized sampling.
- **Curriculum learning:** starting training on simpler, more stable environments (for example, highly liquid instruments, calm periods) and gradually introducing more challenging regimes (illiquid names, crisis periods).

Curriculum schedules can be encoded as rules in the buffer or environment manager, or as explicit training phases with different environment configurations.

Scaling Across Assets and Strategies

In a multi-asset, multi-strategy firm, you may have:

- Separate RL policies for different asset classes or execution styles.
- Shared components (for example, value networks or feature encoders) across policies.

The training plane can support this by:

- Allowing multiple experiments to share environment infrastructure and data.
- Versioning models and configuration independently per strategy.
- Providing resource scheduling (for example, cluster queues) to allocate GPUs/CPUs across experiments.

This is where integration with broader machine learning platforms and cluster managers (such as Kubernetes or internal batch systems) becomes important.

Model Registry and Deployment Workflow

Between the training and serving planes sits the model registry, a controlled repository of trained policies and their metadata.

Model Registry as a Source of Truth

Each trained policy version should be stored in the registry along with:

- Model parameters (weights, architecture).
- Training data range and environment configuration.
- Code and feature pipeline versions.
- Evaluation metrics across backtests and online experiments.
- Governance metadata: approvals, intended mandates, and risk limits.

The registry acts as the *single source of truth* for what is allowed to be deployed. Serving infrastructure does not pull ad hoc models from researchers' directories; it only loads models promoted to specific deployment stages (for example, shadow, canary, full).

Promotion and Rollback

A typical promotion workflow might be:

- A new model is trained and registered as a *candidate* version.
- Automated checks verify integrity (schema compatibility, absence of obvious bugs).
- The model is deployed to *shadow* mode only; online logs and diagnostics are collected.
- If results are satisfactory and governance approvals obtained, it is promoted to *canary* deployment for a slice of flow.
- After further validation, it may be promoted to *primary* for a given strategy.

At each step, the previous primary version remains available for rapid rollback. Rollback is implemented as a configuration change in the serving plane, not an emergency code deployment.

Serving Plane: Low-Latency and Robust Inference

The serving plane connects trained RL policies to live trading. Its design must satisfy both *latency* and *reliability* constraints.

Latency Requirements by Use Case

Not all RL applications require the same latency:

- **Strategic allocation** (for example, daily portfolio rebalancing) might tolerate latencies of seconds or more, since decisions are infrequent.
- **Intra-day execution** (for example, slicing orders in a VWAP schedule) may require latency in the single-digit millisecond range.
- **Order-book-level routing or market making** can demand sub-millisecond responses to remain competitive.

Architectural choices—hardware placement, serialization formats, model complexity—must be tuned to the tightest latency budget the policy must meet.

Inference Service Design

A typical inference service:

- Exposes an API (often over a fast internal protocol) that accepts state features and returns actions.
- Is stateless with respect to long-term data: it retrieves policy parameters at startup and caches them in memory.
- May maintain short-term session or episode context, especially for sequence-based policies, but this state is tightly scoped and recoverable.

To minimize latency and jitter:

- Keep the request path simple: avoid unnecessary network hops or RPC layers.
- Use lightweight serialization (for example, binary formats) and careful memory management.
- Prefer CPU inference for simpler models at very low latency, reserving GPUs for heavier models or batch scenarios.

Model quantization (for example, using reduced-precision arithmetic) and architecture pruning can often reduce inference time without materially affecting policy quality, especially when combined with careful validation.

Co-Location and Network Considerations

For ultra-low-latency use cases, the physical location of inference servers matters:

- **Co-location with exchanges or brokers** minimizes network round-trip times. In many markets, trading firms deploy inference boxes in the same data centers as matching engines or broker gateways.
- **Edge vs. central serving:** you might maintain lightweight inference services at the edge for time-critical decisions and richer, slower analytics centrally.

Network failures and congestion are inevitable. The serving plane should therefore:

- Have health checks that verify connectivity to market data, order gateways, and risk engines.
- Fail safe: in the presence of degraded connectivity, reduce or disable RL-driven flow, falling back to baseline strategies.

Integration with Risk and Order Systems

As discussed earlier in the chapter, RL policies do not send orders to exchanges directly. The serving plane must integrate with:

- **Order gateways:** components that translate policy actions into concrete orders, respecting protocol details and exchange-specific rules.
- **Risk engines:** pre-trade checks that enforce limits and block or modify unsafe instructions.
- **Monitoring and logging:** systems that capture inputs, actions, and outcomes for surveillance and analysis.

This integration is one reason to keep the inference service as a well-encapsulated component: it should not be entangled with order-routing logic or risk checks, which have their own governance.

Reliability, Capacity Planning, and Testing

Beyond latency, the serving plane must be robust under stress and recoverable from failures.

Capacity Planning and Scaling

You should estimate and provision capacity based on:

- Expected peak request rates (for example, around the open and close).
- Worst-case burst patterns (for example, during volatility spikes or macro events).
- Headroom for canary rollouts and shadow policies that add inference load without adding flow.

Scaling patterns include:

- **Horizontal scaling:** multiple inference instances behind a low-latency load balancer. Useful for resilience and moderate-latency applications.
- **Vertical scaling:** high-performance single instances for the tightest latency budgets, with active-passive failover rather than round-robin load balancing.

Deployment Patterns and Rollback

Safe and predictable deployments are essential, particularly under regulatory scrutiny. Common patterns include:

- **Blue/green deployments:** two identical production environments (blue and green). New versions are deployed to the idle one, tested, and then traffic is switched atomically.
- **Progressive rollouts:** gradually increasing the fraction of flow handled by a new version, with automated rollbacks if metrics degrade.

Configuration flags, not code changes, should control which model version is active for a given strategy and account. This simplifies audit trails and enables instant reversion.

Testing Frameworks: Latency, Chaos, and Recovery

Finally, you should test not only the nominal behavior of the serving plane but also its response to failures and stress:

- **Latency benchmarks:** synthetic workloads that measure end-to-end response times under realistic request patterns.
- **Chaos experiments:** deliberately injecting failures (for example, killing instances, introducing network delays) to ensure the system fails safe and recovers cleanly.
- **Disaster-recovery drills:** simulating data-center outages or connectivity losses, validating that fallback paths (for example, to baseline strategies in other regions) work as intended.

These tests should be regular and automated, forming part of the continuous assurance that the RL stack remains reliable as it evolves.

Reinforcement learning for trading is not just a matter of clever algorithms. It requires an architecture that can:

- Serve consistent, leakage-free data and realistic environments.
- Train complex policies efficiently over large historical and simulated datasets.
- Deploy and operate those policies in live markets with tight latency and reliability requirements.
- Connect naturally to governance, monitoring, and risk controls.

By organizing the stack into clear data, training, and serving planes—and by investing in model registries, low-latency inference services, and robust testing frameworks—firms can turn RL prototypes into production systems that are both powerful and trustworthy. In the final section of this chapter, we will examine how to summarize and attribute the performance of these systems in a way that is interpretable for portfolio managers, risk committees, and regulators.

6.5 Performance and Attribution Reporting

So far in this chapter we have focused on *building* RL strategies (through careful backtests), *deploying* them safely (through online experiments and drift monitoring), and *governing* them (through controls and model approval). The final element is to make their behavior *understandable* and *assessable* to the people who ultimately bear responsibility for the risks: portfolio managers, execution heads, risk committees, and regulators.

Those stakeholders usually do not want to see learning curves or loss functions. They want to know:

- How much did this strategy earn or lose, and with what risk?

- What drove those results: allocation, selection, timing, venue choice, or something else?
- How does its behavior vary across market regimes and client mandates?
- How confident can we be that the performance is robust and not a fluke?

This section defines a metric and attribution toolkit that translates the raw behavior of an RL policy into this language. We treat portfolio-level RL and execution RL in parallel, emphasizing where their reporting needs overlap and where they differ.

Core Risk and Performance Metrics

We begin with a common vocabulary for performance and risk. For RL, as for any trading strategy, these metrics should be computed consistently across three contexts:

- Backtests and temporal cross-validation.
- Online experiments (shadow and canary phases).
- Full production deployment.

P&L and Risk over Multiple Horizons

The first layer is P&L and its variability:

- **P&L time series.** Daily or intraday P&L, depending on the strategy's horizon. For execution agents, it is often more natural to measure P&L per order or per basket rather than per day.
- **Volatility.** Standard deviation of P&L over a chosen horizon. For portfolios, you might consider both daily volatility and longer-horizon volatility (for example, monthly), to capture different risk perspectives.

- **Drawdowns.** Peak-to-trough declines in cumulative P&L or equity curve. Maximum drawdown, as well as the distribution of drawdown sizes and durations, is particularly intuitive for risk committees.

Alongside absolute metrics, benchmark-relative metrics matter:

- For portfolio RL, excess return and tracking error versus a benchmark index or policy portfolio.
- For execution RL, cost savings relative to a baseline algorithm (for example, a standard VWAP or TWAP) or to historical desk behavior.

Risk-Adjusted Performance Measures

Headline performance must be scaled by risk. Common ratios include:

- **Sharpe ratio.** Average excess return divided by volatility. This is standard but can be misleading for skewed or fat-tailed strategies.
- **Sortino or downside-adjusted ratios.** Similar to Sharpe but penalizing only downside volatility or tail losses, which often aligns better with risk appetite.
- **Tail-risk measures.** Value-at-risk (VaR), expected shortfall (ES), or other tail metrics computed on the P&L distribution, to quantify extreme event exposure.

For short-horizon RL agents (for example, execution over minutes or hours), these risk-adjusted metrics can be computed per-order or per-episode, then aggregated across orders and time.

Turnover, Costs, and Capacity

An RL policy's headline Sharpe is meaningless if it requires unrealistic turnover, hidden costs, or unscalable capacity. Key metrics include:

- **Turnover.** Fraction of the portfolio traded per period. High turnover often implies higher transaction costs and operational risk.

- **Transaction costs.** Explicit costs (commissions, fees, taxes) and implicit costs (bid-ask spread, market impact). These should be estimated both ex-ante (from models) and ex-post (from realized execution).
- **Participation and capacity.** For execution agents, average and peak participation rates in the market's traded volume; for portfolios, estimates of the maximum capital that could be deployed before costs or impact degrade performance materially.

Because RL strategies often discover subtle edges, their raw gross performance can be modest. Without careful accounting for costs and capacity, reports can overstate their economic relevance.

Execution-Focused Metrics

Execution RL agents require a slightly different lens. Their primary output is *execution quality* rather than directional P&L.

Implementation Shortfall and Benchmark Slippage

Implementation shortfall (IS) measures the difference between the theoretical return of trading at a benchmark price (often arrival price) and the actual return given realized execution prices and costs. For each order or basket:

- Compute the notional P&L if the order had been filled instantly at the benchmark.
- Compute the actual realized P&L given fills, prices, and fees.
- The difference (normalized by notional) is implementation shortfall in basis points.

Likewise, for VWAP and TWAP strategies, you can compute *slippage* versus the day's volume-weighted or time-weighted average price. Reporting should include:

- Average and distribution of IS or slippage by instrument, order size, urgency, and volatility regime.

- Comparisons versus the baseline algorithm or broker, both overall and conditionally.

These metrics tie directly to typical execution mandates and make it easy to judge whether the RL agent is delivering tangible value.

Fill Ratios and Venue Quality

Execution quality is not just about price; it is also about whether and how orders are filled:

- **Fill ratios.** Fraction of order quantity filled, time to first fill, and time to full completion. Poor fill ratios may reflect overly passive behavior or misestimation of liquidity.
- **Venue-level metrics.** For each venue (exchange or internalization mechanism), average slippage, fill probability, and adverse selection (price movement after the fill). An RL agent that dynamically routes flow should be judged on how well it exploits venue differences.

Summaries by venue are particularly important for compliance and best-execution reviews, as they show that venue decisions are based on measured outcomes rather than opaque heuristics.

Attribution for Portfolio RL

Risk managers and portfolio managers want to know *why* a portfolio-level RL strategy earned its returns. Traditional performance attribution decomposes return into *allocation*, *selection*, and *timing* effects. We can adapt this to RL.

Allocation, Selection, and Timing

Informally:

- **Allocation effect** captures value added by choosing which asset classes, sectors, or factors to overweight or underweight relative to a benchmark.

- **Selection effect** measures value from choosing specific instruments within a given bucket (for example, stock-picking within a sector).
- **Timing effect** reflects gains or losses from changing positions over time, even if average allocations match the benchmark.

For an RL portfolio policy, you can compute attribution over a chosen horizon by:

- Defining a benchmark or neutral portfolio (for example, index weights, or a static 60/40 mix).
- For each time period, decomposing the return difference between the RL portfolio and the benchmark into allocation and selection components using standard attribution formulas.
- Attributing residual effects to timing, particularly when the RL policy actively shifts exposures in response to state variables.

These components can then be aggregated by sector, factor, region, or other dimensions. The resulting bar charts and tables speak directly to how portfolio managers typically think about skill.

Factor- and Signal-Based Attribution

Because RL policies often condition on feature sets that resemble traditional alpha signals (value, momentum, quality, etc.), it is natural to examine:

- **Factor exposures over time.** Regressing portfolio returns on a set of risk factors reveals whether the RL policy is effectively tilting towards known sources of return (for example, small-cap, value) or creating new, unexplained exposures.
- **Signal-conditioned P&L.** Grouping states or trades by relevant signals (for example, volatility, carry, trend strength) and summarizing P&L within each group shows where the policy is making or losing money.

This type of attribution helps stakeholders understand whether the RL agent is "rediscovering" traditional factors or capturing something genuinely new—and whether that something is stable across regimes.

Attribution for Execution RL

Execution agents also benefit from attribution, but their levers differ: venue choice, order type, schedule, and aggression level.

Decomposing Execution Performance

You can decompose implementation shortfall or cost savings into:

- **Venue effect.** Compare realized performance under the RL venue mix to a counterfactual using an alternative venue distribution (for example, the baseline's mix) while holding other decisions fixed.
- **Order-type effect.** Assess the contribution from choosing different order types (market, limit, iceberg, pegged) by evaluating their average performance in similar contexts.
- **Scheduling effect.** Evaluate how the intra-order time profile (front-loaded vs. back-loaded execution) affects market impact and slippage.

Practically, you approximate these counterfactuals using historical data and models: for example, "What would have been the average slippage if we had used the baseline's venue and order-type choices for orders with similar size, volatility, and spread?"

Breaking performance down this way reveals whether the RL agent's edge comes primarily from better venue selection, smarter timing, or improved order-type usage. It also surfaces potential regressions: an agent might gain on schedule but lose on venue choice, or vice versa.

State-Conditional and Regime-Conditional Reporting

A single global Sharpe ratio or average implementation shortfall can hide important structure. RL strategies are inherently stateful: they adapt behavior based on volatility, liquidity, time-of-day, and other variables. Performance reporting should mirror this.

Slicing by Market Regime

Using indicators from earlier sections (for example, realized volatility, liquidity metrics, factor regimes), you can define coarse regimes such as:

- Low, medium, and high volatility.
- Normal vs. stressed liquidity.
- Risk-on vs. risk-off factor environments.

For each regime, compute:

- Average and distribution of P&L, risk-adjusted performance, and drawdowns.
- Execution metrics (IS, slippage, fill ratios) for execution agents.
- Action-distribution statistics (for example, average aggression, turnover) to show how the policy adapts.

These slices help answer questions like "Does the RL strategy behave sensibly in crises?" or "Is its edge confined to calm markets?"

Slicing by Internal State and Constraints

In addition to external regimes, the policy's *internal* state—inventory, risk utilization, proximity to limits—affects decisions. Reporting may include:

- P&L and costs when inventory is high vs. low, or when risk utilization is near limits.
- Behavior and performance when the kill-switches or soft limits discussed earlier are active.

Such slices reveal whether the RL agent is using risk capacity efficiently and whether constraints are binding in a way that distorts behavior.

Communicating Uncertainty and Multiple-Testing Risk

Stakeholders are rightly skeptical of performance claims derived from complex models. Two common pitfalls are overconfidence in point estimates and hidden multiple-testing.

Confidence Intervals and Stability Checks

Rather than quoting a single Sharpe ratio or cost saving, you should:

- Provide confidence intervals or error bars based on appropriate statistical models (for example, accounting for autocorrelation in returns).
- Report metrics across multiple time splits (for example, different years, different market regimes) to show stability or instability.
- Include simple visualizations such as rolling Sharpe ratios or rolling cost savings over time.

If performance is highly concentrated in a short window or a single regime, that should be made explicit; RL does not exempt you from the need for robust evidence.

Multiple-Testing and Data-Snooping

RL workflows often involve many design choices: feature sets, reward functions, architectures, training curricula. Even if you did not consciously "p-hack" the results, the sheer number of choices can make good outcomes more likely by chance.

To mitigate this:

- Be transparent about how many candidate models or reward formulations were tried.
- Use hold-out test periods, as discussed earlier in the chapter, and clearly label any metrics that were used in model selection.
- Avoid over-interpretation of fine-grained slices with few observations; instead, focus on broader patterns that are supported by ample data.

Explaining these limitations does not weaken the case for your RL strategy; it strengthens credibility by showing that you understand the statistical risks.

Toward a Standard "Model Factsheet"

To bring these ideas together, many institutions find it useful to define a standard *model factsheet* for each RL strategy. While formats differ, a typical factsheet includes:

- **Mandate and role.** Plain-language description of what the RL policy does, its horizon, and its constraints.
- **Summary metrics.** Key performance and risk statistics over relevant horizons (for example, annualized return, volatility, Sharpe, maximum drawdown, turnover, transaction costs, capacity).
- **Benchmark and baseline comparisons.** Excess performance versus benchmark portfolios or baseline execution algorithms.
- **Attribution views.** Allocation/selection/timing decomposition for portfolios; venue/order-type/scheduling contributions for execution.
- **Regime-conditional behavior.** Performance and action summaries across volatility, liquidity, and factor regimes.
- **Uncertainty and robustness.** Confidence intervals, stability across time, and discussion of any known weaknesses or fragile conditions.
- **Governance hooks.** Model version, approval status, applicable kill-switch triggers, and linkage to the model registry.

Because the format is standardized, risk managers and committees can compare different RL approaches side by side, and they know where to look for answers to common questions. For the RL team, factsheets also serve as an internal discipline, forcing clarity about what a given policy is actually doing and how convincingly it has been validated.

Performance and attribution reporting is the final layer that makes RL strategies intelligible and governable. A well-designed reporting toolkit:

- Translates complex, stateful policies into familiar metrics for P&L, risk, and execution quality.
- Decomposes outcomes into meaningful drivers—allocation, selection, timing, venue, schedule—so that stakeholders can judge whether the agent is adding value in the intended ways.
- Shows how behavior and performance vary across regimes and internal states, rather than hiding everything behind a single Sharpe ratio.
- Communicates uncertainty and acknowledges multiple-testing risks, building trust through transparency.

Together with rigorous backtesting, cautious online experimentation, strong governance, and robust system architecture, such reporting closes the loop: it allows reinforcement learning to move from research labs into production trading in a way that satisfies both quantitative ambitions and institutional responsibilities.

www.ingramcontent.com/pod-product-compliance
Lightning Source LLC
LaVergne TN
LVHW022154200926
848481LV00006B/1747
* 9 7 9 8 8 9 6 6 5 2 3 0 4 *